OUTSIDE
INSIDE

Decorating in the Natural Style

OUTSIDE
Decorating in the Natural Style
INSIDE

BARBARA ARIA

PHOTOGRAPHS BY
STEVE MOORE

Thames and Hudson

A RUNNING HEADS BOOK

1992 Copyright © by Running Heads Incorporated

The photographs on pages 19, 41, 60, 75, 102–103, and 140 are used courtesy of Villegas Editores Files–Colombia.

First published in the United States in 1992 by
Thames and Hudson Inc., 500 Fifth Avenue,
New York, New York 10110

OUTSIDE INSIDE
was conceived and produced by
Running Heads Incorporated
55 West 21 Street
New York, NY 10010

Library of Congress Catalog Card Number 92-80100

Creative Director: Linda Winters
Editor: Rose K. Phillips
Designer: Jan Melchior
Managing Editor: Jill Hamilton
Production Associate: Belinda Hellinger

Typeset by Trufont Typographers, Inc.
Color separations by Hong Kong Scanner Craft Co., Ltd.
Printed and bound in Singapore by Tien Wah Press (Pte.) Ltd.

Acknowledgments

Many thanks to all those who helped in the making of this book, and in particular to the designers, furniture makers, handcrafters, gardeners, and cooks who in partnership with nature created the work that fills these pages. My special thanks also to the many individuals who graciously welcomed us, and the cameras, into their homes; and to the businesses and organizations who made products available to us for photography, or who helped facilitate the photography of locations. Wind chimes by Zona and a whirligig by Wolfman, Gold and Good Company were especially appreciated and appear on page 94, and Simes Herbes Co. provided the edible flowers pictured on pages 102–103.

I am, of course, indebted to Marta Hallett and Ellen Milionis of Running Heads, Inc., for their origination and support of this project, and to Jamie Camplin and Susan Dwyer at Thames and Hudson, who made it possible; to Rose K. Phillips, my editor, and to everyone else at Running Heads whose energies contributed to its successful completion; to Jan Melchior for her skillful book design; and to Cornelia Guest for her calm determination in organizing the location photography. In addition, the following designers, architects, and artisans—all leaders in the natural design movement—generously permitted us to photograph their work and homes: Armscote Manor Dried Flowers (pages 76, 84 left), Benincasa & McGowan (pages 63, 81 bottom, 130), Centerbrook (pages 96, 97), Alejandro Cabo (pages 19 left, 61 top), Paul Chilkov (page 98), Clodagh Architectural Designs (pages 46–47, 62 top, 98, 99, 125), Damien Dewing of Atelier (pages 56, 62, 66), Mikael Elkan (page 65 right top and bottom), Mary Emmerling (pages 16, 65 left), Jerry Farrell (page 49), Indoor Garden Room (pages 75, 82), Roderick James (pages 11, 25, 26–27, 44, 50, 134), Wendy Stuart Kaplan (pages 40, 52–53, 69, 85, 87, 90, 136), Simon Lycett (pages 76, 84 left), Daniel Mack (pages 13, 18, 34 top and bottom, 61, 65 top and bottom), Bob Patino (pages 58, 59, 121), Robert Pierpont (pages 62, 135), Martin Robinson (pages 45, 55, 75, 78, 82, 93 bottom, 132–133), and the Selslea Herb Farm (15, 74, 77, 80, 84 right, 106). Benjamin Villegas provided outstanding additional photographs from the Villegas Editores Files which were used on pages 19 (left and right), 41, 51, 60 (top and bottom), 73, 102–103, and 140. I am also grateful to many friends, both in the United States and in England, who gave so generously of their time and efforts and made many invaluable suggestions: in particular, Sally Hawkins, Yva Bernard, Sue Broude, Mayo Petersson, and Pam Margionelli—thanks.

CONTENTS

INTRODUCTION

Old Man said, "Ah," and smiled as he looked at the earth,

for she was very beautiful—

truly the most beautiful thing he had made so far.

—NATIVE AMERICAN CREATION MYTH,
JAMAICA HIGHWATER,
ANPAO:
AN AMERICAN INDIAN ODYSSEY

NORSE SAGAS TELL HOW THE Scandinavians of old would build their homes around a living tree. Worshippers of nature and its vast mysteries, they believed that a house should be "rooted" in the land on which it stood. With a tree growing green through the midst of their domestic lives, its roots spreading deep into the earth beneath their floors, the Norse people were perpetually reminded not only of the endless regeneration of life, but also of the unity of all living things.

During the past century, Western life-styles have moved further and further away from a partnership with nature. The English word *civilized* is virtually synonymous with the idea of human life as separate from and dominant over nature, while the "sophistication" to which we so aspire embodies an abandonment of all that is natural.

Whether our culture's rift with nature began with our gradual abandonment of the gods and goddesses of crops, wind, water, and so on, or more abruptly with the beginnings of the industrial revolution, the more advanced Western civilization has become, the more we have lost contact with the rhythm of the natural world in our daily lives. The modern period in architecture and interior design in many ways celebrated this very detachment from the natural world outside our doors, paying homage to the new materials, implements, and techniques made possible by twentieth-century technology. Besides, the urban world had been suddenly lit up with electricity—described at the time as "man's triumph over night"; movement at what seemed like unbelievably high speeds was altering perceptions of time and space; and everything that was new suggested that mankind had entered a radically different era having nothing to do with the past. With modernism, domestic design deserted its roots in the natural world.

Modern life in general meant a liberation from many forms of drudgery—tasks that, nevertheless, had once put us in touch with nature. Finally, thanks to plastics and poured concrete, washing machines and electric stoves, we were emancipated from tree, rock, stream, and fire. Home became, in the words of the architect Le Corbusier, a "machine for living," a factory in which life could be lived efficiently. One of the early proponents of the International Style, the Dutch architect J. P. Oud, wrote in an essay of the need for "cleanliness and order, for standardization and repetition, for per-

The slack curve of a string hammock, previous page, suggests lazy afternoons on the porch. Birch logs, above, have long been used as rustic furnishings, as in this "barnhouse" in Devon, England, opposite.

fection and high finish." Our homes became streamlined, pared down, devoid of decoration—sometimes very beautifully, very gracefully, as attested to by such masterpieces as Mies Van der Rohe's timeless and virtually transparent Farnsworth House in Chicago, which pays homage to the landscape in which it sits. Yet, in the formulaic works of lesser architects especially, modernism—which flourished during the 1920s and '30s and influenced generations of architects thereafter—has cost us our link with the natural world in all its unbridled diversity.

We're not the first generation to contemplate what we have lost in the name of progress. In the eighteenth century, Jean-Jacques Rousseau and his followers wondered what their society—the rationalistic society of Newton and Locke—might have lost through its search for order, predictability, and material gain. They were the first in the history of Western civilization to look longingly at the mud huts and grass skirts of "barbaric" peoples. Historically, both home and garden had been valued as safe refuge from the threatening unknown of the wilderness beyond—the tamer and

more formal they were, the safer they seemed. But by now science had explained many of the mysteries of nature, and the wilderness seemed less threatening.

Rousseau, probably the most prophetic thinker of his era, advocated a movement away from formal gardens toward nature untamed, and made a strong case for rusticity and primitivism as antidotes to the spiritless life-styles that he saw around him. A short while later, reaction to the problems of urbanism spawned the first "back to nature" movement in design, with rustic garden furniture and less landscaped designs gaining widespread popularity. William Robinson's immensely influential text *The Wild Garden* followed in the next century, touting the glory of nature when it is left to its own devices.

Today, a new generation of architects working in a "natural style," such as British architect David Sellars—whose plan for a "satellite village" calls for a walk through parkland as a necessary part of the daily trip from home to work—believe as Rousseau did that our detachment from nature has far-reaching implications. Because we live in environments in which we are deprived of natural experiences,

The design of this contemporary house in upstate New York, opposite, which was built largely with materials from the surrounding land, encompasses an indoor "porch" and "garden" complete with a fruit-producing grape vine and a flower bed. In a tree-surrounded Connecticut home, below, a rustic table and its miniature companion with one forked foot complement the curves of earthenware bowls.

Garden views, combined with greenery tumbling from an iron plant stand and antique furnishings made from natural materials, bring the outside into the sunroom of this London townhouse, left overleaf. An antique watering can emphasizes the gardenesque quality of the room. At Selslea Herb Farm in the English Cotswolds, right overleaf, a copper coal scuttle serves as an unusual container for an abundance of flowers, grasses, and herbs that have been brought indoors and dried.

the current theory goes, we make poor decisions regarding the life of the planet.

Ever since the eighteenth century, when Rousseau first sounded his trumpet of alarm, we have grown preoccupied with material consumption, gradually abandoning our link with the materials available outside our doors. As society grew more highly civilized and urbanized, we moved toward specialization and away from home production. Wealthy homeowners of the late nineteenth and twentieth centuries imported materials from farther afield, rather than using local materials, to signify prestige. This represented the beginning of the conspicuous consumption that reached its height in recent decades. When the new chemical industries of the late nineteenth century made possible the production of synthetic pigments, scents, and surfaces, we embraced that possibility, scarcely thinking that as we filled our homes with laminates and particleboards, polyurethane and plastics, our homes, our health, and even the planet would suffer.

In order to feed our hungry spirits, we've learned to escape to the country or into the garden, to feast our senses on the

A comfortable parlor bedroom, featured at Showhouse 91 on Long Island, New York, above, features a folding screen of woven panels stretched across a frame of unpeeled wood. Topiary adds a touch of gracious formality to an otherwise casual setting. Bringing furniture and ornamental elements traditionally found on porches and patios indoors is an easy and witty way to evoke a natural style.

sights, sounds, and scents of nature. Often unconscious of our own actions, we stroke leaves to feel textures almost foreign to us; bruise them to smell their fragrance; observe moments of hushed silence in order to listen attentively to the sound of a bird, the wind, some stream beyond our vision. We delight in so simple a gesture as picking a blackberry. We look to nature for its ability to show us some meaning and essential order in our lives, as well as for the peace and tranquility that allow us to contemplate that order.

Now, as we approach the turn of the century, new needs and desires push us further in our search for the kind of retreat offered by nature. Instead of finding havens away from home, we are searching for a way of creating home as haven. The interior design and decoration of our homes gives us a framework for our lives, just as our lives shape the way our homes look, smell, feel, and sound. It is human activity in partnership with nature, and the residues of that activity—herbs and flowers hung out to dry, a well-used rake propped against a wall— that lend the farmhouse or the gardener's cottage their inviting air of domestic comfort and intimacy. The way a room is decorated and furnished, in the words of the architectural historian Mario Praz, "mirrors the soul of its occupants."

In this post-industrial age of fax machines, interfaced computer terminals, microwaved meals, and videotaped movies, we are spending more and more time in our houses, whether we're working, resting, eating, or entertaining. Average Westerners may spend 90 percent of their lives indoors. At the same time, our uneasy pact with technology drives us to seek its antithesis whenever and wherever we are able, to find places and moments of repose in the midst of the bleeping, flickering, hard-edged world that we have made for ourselves.

Not surprisingly, many people are looking to the garden both as inspiration and as metaphor. In fact, there is a longstanding connection between garden design and home design, and elements of both environments have been intermingled throughout history. For the plants in a garden to thrive, their requirements for water, nutrients, and light must be met. But they also respond to touch, sound, the air itself. Humans also need a nurturing, hospitable environment

A metal urn whose surface is tempered by years of outdoor use serves as an umbrella stand in this downtown Manhattan loft, above. It would also make a charming ice bucket. With the window open, the grass growing in the Italian terracotta planter waves evocatively in the breeze. Though these decorative touches are few—and inexpensive to achieve— they impart an airy, country atmosphere in even the most citified environments.

if they are to flourish. We need environments that address us as whole people. The home must satisfy the most fundamental needs of those who inhabit it, or all of its stylish beauty will be like seeds thrown on sand, lying fallow. And those needs—more complex even than the needs of plants—are more than purely functional.

There is increasingly a feeling in our society that state-of-the-art kitchens, designer sheets, Breuer chairs, and imported furniture cannot sufficiently furnish the home: that a house is infused with the warmth and vibrancy of a home when there is a link with nature, an interdependence of the man-made and the natural environment. There is a growing awareness of nature's intrinsic worth and beauty—an awareness brought about, in part, by our belated realization that the natural world is both vital to our survival and is itself endangered; that we are a part of nature, partners together in our shared well-being; that we need to enjoy and protect the natural world, whether we live in the city or in the country; that, rather than trying to master nature, we must endeavor to live in harmony with it.

Designing with nature means

moving away from the slick domestic interior of past decades toward a more relaxed style of living that satisfies our cravings for the sensual experiences we have long sought on our country walks. It means learning how to draw from simple sources that are close at hand—those sights, sounds, scents, touches, and tastes that delight the spirit. In many cases, this means blurring the boundaries between indoors and outdoors by incorporating nature into the home.

Not so long ago, labor-saving devices represented an improvement in the quality of life. Today, that quality (together with its new meaning of spiritual and physical health) could be represented by a tree growing indoors, Norse style, or by a comfortable hammock slung across the living room.

In his foreword to artist Andrea Branzi's book of neo-primitive furnishings—chairs made from branches, twigs, sticks of wood—the French critic Pierre Restany speaks of these "objects of domestic functionality" acting upon the human condition as a catalyst for "the quality of life." Branzi's creations, claims Restany, lead us almost magically into a "dream time." They invite contempla-

tion, meditation, imagination. They make us think about the nature of being human in the larger world of nature. Like nature itself, they seem unfinished, suggesting continual growth and change, the continuum.

And yet Branzi's creations speak also of our technological intelligence. Raw materials close at hand are shaped in ancient yet newly remembered ways and

mixed with the best that modern technology has to offer. With a bit of ingenuity, the same harmonious mixture of natural and man-made elements—such as a table and chairs made from willow branches, a desk crafted from pieces of warped beechwood, or a chandelier fashioned entirely from trees—can distinguish the contemporary home.

This magnificently eccentric rustic chair, opposite, with its high back and woven Shaker cotton seat, was fashioned by hand from peeled maple saplings. Its unfinished quality contrasts strikingly with the more conventional furnishings of this Connecticut farmhouse.

Containers crafted from hollowed-out wooden cords retain the natural bends of their branches. They are effectively displayed against marquetry in this New Mexican home, above left. In the same home, above right, a carpet enriched by vegetable dyes and a light-toned wood couch incorporate a natural palette.

From New York to Los Angeles, London to Paris and Sydney, Australia, in city apartments and in country houses, hard edges are being softened with moss and twigs, leaves and grass, wicker and wildflowers. Whether through a simple arrangement of grasses in a sweet-smelling straw basket or a collection of birds' nests, the outdoors is finding its way in and creating a new kind of environment for the '90s and beyond.

Many of these environments are in themselves testaments to the power of sunlight and rain, seasonal change, the forest and the herb garden, the earth itself with its mineral treasures. Others are simply comfortable living environments that preserve some of the peace of the garden, or some of the mystery of wild nature.

Instead of the static environments of recent times, "natural style" environments grow and evolve with the seasons, as nature itself grows and changes. A bucket of country flowers in summer might be replaced by a dried flower arrangement in the winter. Floors covered in rush matting during the hottest part of the year can be re-covered in wool as the days turn cold. In a society where one in nine adults

In this London house, left, an easy flow exists between the garden outdoors and the gardener's studio indoors, which not only is used for the propagation of seedlings and the rooting of cuttings, but also serves as a serene, sunny place in which to sit and plan the garden, or simply to dream. Gardeners' straw hats hang near the door, while an African drum serves as an extra seat.

lives alone, this kind of growing, living presence can be both enriching and comforting. As nineteenth-century garden writer Jane Loudon wrote, "What a difference it makes in the pleasure we have in returning home, if we have something to visit that we know has been improving in our absence."

The new emphasis on "natural" life-styles being developed in the '90s is not so much a change in style as a change in values. Although this book is about bringing nature into the home, and not about the world environment on a grand scale, it is hard in many senses to separate the two. The most obvious examples of their indivisible nature can be found in the "green" architectural projects in progress around the world, in which ancient techniques and those made possible in our technological age are being combined to preserve nonrenewable resources in the natural world. Many of these projects—houses that mirror a plant's integrated system, supplying its parts with air, water, and light—are based on models provided by the latest in computer systems technology.

But, as suggested by the Green movement's new motto, "Think globally, act locally,"

even the smallest gesture made in the interests of nature can help. Many of the ideas in this book that are designed to foster a richer and more fulfilling life-style will also result in a healthier planet and a healthier body. There is a new term in home design, the "sick building syndrome." Some people are finding that they cannot physically tolerate the fumes constantly emitted by the materials used to build and decorate their homes. Bringing nature into the home minimizes the use of those man-made materials that are detrimental to our health.

This book looks back, as well as forward, because the natural, harmonious flow between the outdoor and the indoor worlds reflected in home design and decoration today was once integral to daily living, with nature playing its part in the making of dwellings, the cooking of food, and the decoration of home. Even in our own grandparents' time, logs were burned for warmth, oil extracted from turnip seeds often acted as an inexpensive source of light, and herbs from the garden were routinely hung from the rafters to dry for use during winter months, imparting both color and fragrance to the home.

Twig rocking chairs crafted from materials of the Wisconsin woods, above, are given an up-to-date flavor with the addition of boldly striped pillows. In a tiny Minnesota living room, below, antique iron garden furniture has been paired with a striking wooden farm rake.

Everyday furnishings and implements, too, were fashioned by rural people from materials found outside the door and transformed through the simplest processes—from twigs and branches bent or split; from reeds and rushes woven into chair seats, mats, or baskets; from clay, kneaded and coiled; from iron wrought; from wool or cotton spun and woven into rugs. Materials were few and simple, but they served many purposes. Herbs and flowers, for instance, produced dyes, scents, tastes, and visual delight.

Even today, the yurts of the Asian mountain nomads are built of willow frames covered in felt pressed from the wool of local sheep. The Mbuti pygmies, hunter-gatherers living in the forests of Zaire, make their homes from sticks and leaves, and decorate with sweet-smelling vines, whose strengthening juices they also drink. Color and form, texture and scent, unite the inhabitants with the "mother forest" on whose riches life depends. In many African villages, mud huts are decorated with dyes from the earth, and roofed with twigs and straw. Like birds' nests, these dwellings are one with the surrounding landscape.

On the other hand, bringing raw nature into the home does not represent a retreat into a romanticized past. It means blending what has been lost in our rush toward the future with what we've gained in that rush in terms of the quality of our lives. There is no reason, for instance, why the home computer room should not be decorated with plants, its whir broken by the sound of a wind chime, or the odor of plastic masked with a sweet-smelling potpourri.

For a long time architecture, home design, and decoration in the Western world have been devoted to satisfying the eye. But our richest experiences of the world, and of our homes, are those that awaken and comfort all our senses. Plato defined *chora*, the oldest Greek word for "place," as a receptacle for experience, a "container of feelings." The essence of place, he stated, cannot be experienced rationally, but can only be mediated through sight, sound, smell, taste, and touch—through the evidence of our senses.

Each chapter of this book explores one of the five senses, looking at the ways in which nature, brought indoors in its wild form or minimally manipulated (in the form of rough-hewn wood, spun cotton, or woven straw, for instance), can stimulate and satisfy our needs for sensual experiences.

Many of the interiors in this book have been inspired by the garden, which has always answered to our delight in sensual stimulation. The medieval pleasure garden, in particular, was devoted to this kind of multifaceted experience. In the year 1260, Albert Magnus, a Dominican theologian, wrote his instructions for setting out such a pleasure garden. They included a lawn, like a green cloth, surrounded by such sweet-smelling herbs as rue, sage, and basil, and the flowers violet, columbine, lily, rose, and iris. A broad bench of flowering turf, braced with wattle, would give a soft and fragrant place to sit and drink sweet teas perfumed with garden flowers, while a fountain would introduce the gentle sound of water. Elements of such a multisensual environment can be adapted for the home, particularly in relation to scent, which is the subject of Chapter Three.

The Japanese have long recognized how elements from nature, brought indoors, address the intermingling of the various senses

and the impact that domestic interiors have on us, particularly in their use of colors and textures. Chapters One and Two, on sight and touch, address ways to create such visual and tactile elements in the home.

In China, Taoism has resulted in *Feng Shui*, the sacred art of placement or interior arrangement. *Feng Shui*, meaning "wind and water," sees a fundamental link between earth energy, or *ch'i*, the vital life breath, and the body's own energy. *Ch'i* is carried by air, light, earth, and water. Designers working in the tradition of *Feng Shui* in China, and increasingly in the West, compose room arrangements that encourage a good flow of energy. When rearrangement is not practical, plants, wind chimes, and other natural elements are used to counteract bad *ch'i*. A basket of dried flowers might be placed on top of a wardrobe in a high-ceilinged room, for instance, to stop the eye (and its related energy) from travelling upward where it would get lost in the empty space above. In a railroad apartment with a succession of doors leading the eye straight through and out the other end, hanging

Tumbling ivy adds a touch of the wild to a highly cultivated alcove in a New England hallway, above.
The restful, variegated green of its leaves echoes the leaf green in the floral curtain that serves as a backdrop to the plant.

plants or crystals in the doorways allow the eye to rest, preserving energy. Or a group of stones might be arranged on a window ledge to focus the eye, stopping the outward flow of *ch'i*.

Within this book, many types of interior "landscape" are represented. The sparse Japanese-style room and the room shaped according to the principles of *Feng Shui* are two distinctive examples. There are also more familiar settings: an Adirondack cabin with its log furniture and rustic lamps, a "garden" study in London filled with botanical accessories, and a country cottage decorated with wicker and greenery. All bring the outdoors in and celebrate the sensuality of the natural world.

The warm glow of wood is complemented by the variegated greens of plants, rug, and lamp shades, opposite. The running deer and giant pine cones on the impressive log mantelpiece, as well as the basket brimming with cones on the hearth, recall a woodland environment. A barn-studio designed by a Devonshire architect for his wife, a quiltmaker, was constructed entirely from Douglas fir, right. The massive portal was inspired by traditional barn doors.

Chapter One

VIEW
THE OUTSIDE
IN

Nature is beautiful because it is sentient.

—LE CORBUSIER

THE PERCEPTION OF NATURE AS beautiful is universal. Through the ages poets have repeatedly praised visual phenomena in the natural world—the glory of lofty peaks and crashing waves, the pleasures of tree, lake, and meadow, the simple beauty of a lily or a bamboo stem. While tastes in architecture, dress, music, painting, and even body physique have passed through their myriad changes, the appreciation of nature's wonders has remained constant.

As we race headlong into the twenty-first century, visual taste seems more than ever before to be governed by that age-old longing for sensations that are capable of sparking our most fundamental memories—those same sensations of which the poets have sung since ancient times. It is common wisdom that the sight of natural forms can cure an ailing spirit—a belief that has been validated by recent findings in environmental psychology. Studies suggest that viewing natural scenes produces in the human brain higher levels of alpha waves than does viewing man-made or urban scenes. The presence of alpha waves is associated with wakeful relaxation and triggers feelings of elation, friendliness, and well-being. It is now believed that our universal appreciation of nature evolved over a period of more than a million years, years during which our ancestors lived in a natural setting, working with nature for the survival of the species. Our senses are, in essence, evolutionarily adapted to respond to nature. We prefer to seek out organic forms with which to surround ourselves and feel most at ease when we are in contact with them, because they are in some way familiar to us—even if we have never met them before. Although a work of art or design may defy our cultural sense of aesthetics, we seem to have an inherent understanding of the complex structure of nature, and an innate ability to comprehend and enjoy even the most complexly structured of natural forms.

It's not surprising, then, that the impulse to bring the sights of nature indoors purely to delight the eye is an ancient one. For hundreds of years, during which the vast wilderness beyond garden walls seemed threateningly chaotic, the garden itself was brought indoors. Out of necessity, gardens were planted primarily for sustenance, but whenever possible they also provided visual delights that could effortlessly make the transition into the home. For example, roses and violets were woven into garlands in medieval times.

A collection of decoys ornaments this rambling home, previous page.
Simple delights—a birds' nest and honeysuckle—nestle against a pantry window,
above. A London conservatory serves as an extension of the garden, opposite.

A Timeless Philosophy

This willow table and chairs set is displayed in a dining room, above. Willow branches were lined up side by side and covered with glass to form the top of the table.

In the 1800s, the English *cottage orné*—a fanciful summer house—became a popular setting in which to stage outdoor scenes indoors, for by now the main house was too formal and refined to allow for such impetuosities as garlands or branches. In one such cottage, built on the grounds of Killeton House in Devon, walls were covered in bark and in woven matting intricately patterned with pinecones, halved and nailed. Ingeniously, branches were bent into gothic arches. Here was a comfortable place, defined by its rusticity as a retreat, where one could escape from the stiff social conventions of the time.

Only the means have varied for expressing that perennial impulse to include nature in the visual settings for our lives. Even modernism, generally seen as the antithesis of all things natural because of its concrete and glass, never was meant to entirely banish nature from the home. Modernist texts make it clear that the use of glass and plastics, with their transparent qualities, was in fact intended to put the indoor life of people and the outdoor life of nature into a closer relationship.

Before modernism, the Victorians had tried to bring nature indoors by reproducing it in a highly realistic fashion on textiles and prints, and by creating elaborately detailed renditions of natural forms on ironwork and woodwork. This was nature idealized, while nature proper was left safely out of doors. It must have been a liberating experience when, with the advent of modernism, it became possible, even fashionable, to sit inside one's living room surrounded by views of the land beyond. This was nature itself, no reproduction: but it was still outside, neatly framed and separated by a pane of glass.

This "outdoor" scene, above, is actually indoors in a Colombia, South America, residence. Native plant species, a stone water trough, and a garden lamp fixture create an oasis environment and a cool refuge from the hot climate. Rustic overhead beams in natural tones further establish a connection with the outdoors.

Today, the sights of the natural world are literally being brought indoors—mushrooms, moss, and all. Nature is now embraced in every corner of every room, and it is being put to use in a huge variety of ways, both decorative and functional. In the case of a water sculpture, a giant nautilus shell, or a six-foot spiral moss topiary, nature becomes decorative art. It can be furniture—a chair made of willow branches, a folding screen of grasses stretched across a bamboo frame—or it can be an accessory such as a basket made from crinkly autumn leaves, a moss-encrusted clay pot, or a forked branch coat stand. When walls are covered in grass or bark cloth, or the kitchen counter is paved with the variegated grays of fieldstone, nature becomes fully integrated into the home. Even the state-of-the-art electronic grandfather clock in the hallway might be nature brought indoors: Michigan artist Clifton Monteith has designed a skeletal version of the classic clock with an aspen board for a spine, ribs of bent willow, a birch bark face, and numbers marked by willow dowels.

In some examples, nature is right outside the window, and bringing it in creates an effortless

A Natural Phenomenon

A metal container originally intended for use in the greenhouse was covered with large, crinkly autumn leaves. It acts as unique storage for letters and magazine cuttings in this garden-like London home office, opposite. The office itself, above, occupies one corner of a conservatory— an excellent example of combining natural elements with furnishings. The nature theme introduced by abundant plants is echoed in the grape-motif screen, the wicker chair, and the wooden wardrobe painted to resemble bamboo.

transition between two worlds. In California's Napa Valley, for instance, a vineyard owner has taken large and interesting boulders from her land and brought them into her house for use as sculpture. A Maine couple scavenges the nearby Atlantic shoreline in search of potential decorative objects. In their home, unbleached cotton hangs from lengths of driftwood, curtaining the windows of an oceanside bedroom furnished with a driftwood bed and a bedside table roughly cut from natural local stone.

Nature is sometimes brought from further afield to create a separate refuge. In a narrow London hallway, a branch propped against a wall nestles a bird's nest in its crook. In a Philadelphia living room that doubles as a Mediterranean herb garden, French lavender moves in the breeze from an open window that looks out onto city streets. In every case, these are re-creations of sights that have been found pleasing in natural surroundings, and they contain that same curious, enticing blend of serenity and vivacity found in nature.

Perhaps the impulse to bring nature indoors in the most literal sense—rather than to represent it pictorially as the Victorians did, or to frame it in glass—is so vital today because we have been surrounded in our daily lives by objects that have been conceived, designed, and made by others in one style or another. Inevitably, a human presence speaks from a man-made object. In the case of mass-produced objects this presence is an anonymous babble, and the "designer" objects pervading homes almost shout.

By contrast, objects from nature—free from the touch and mind of others—are, in a sense, silent presences. The same holds true, to a lesser degree, for products that have been made from natural materials close to their original state. A chair made from branches, though the product of a person's imagination and labor, is nevertheless shaped primarily by the branches themselves. It is virtually an artless object; the art, the modification of things by human skill, stands opposed to nature. The graceful contours of a willow chair are a creation not so much of the craftsperson's design skill, but of the inherent flexibility and tension of wet willow as it responds to the pressure of a hand sensitive to its qualities, and of the craftsperson's skill and reverence in harvesting it.

An eccentric loveseat, above, and weathered wood, Santa Fe-style side table, below, owe their charm to their rustic origins. The seat was made from a peeled maple fork and has a Shaker woven cotton covering.

The natural style is identified with certain qualities of form, line, and color present in nature, and with the materials of nature themselves. It is a visual evocation of life outside in the natural world, and as such it can be found in happy coexistence with any one of a number of interior furnishing styles, or it can become a style of its own.

In a Pacific Northwest house, a display of sculptural, almost luminously silvered driftwood and delicate, bare branches softens a corner of the living room, adding to the light, spacious feel created by rough-plastered walls, pickled floors, and unbleached cotton cushion covers—a look that echoes the open, fluid feeling of the beach-scape outside. There is nothing static here; the display changes with the seasons and with the mood of the day. Many of the rooms created in a natural style exist in a process of growth, evolving like nature itself. Even the ever-changing interplay of natural light and shadow can evoke the outdoors in a room. Placing light catchers—such as pendant prismatic crystals and shimmery marbles anchoring flowers in a clear vase—in strategic locations dramatizes the presence of sunlight.

A sturdy log bed accessorized with tartan emphasizes the rugged quality of this log house in rural New York, above.

The bedside "tree" lamp fixture beside a dish of spicy potpourri blends perfectly with the woodsy feel of this bedroom.

The owners of this whitewashed, barn-style home have adorned the walls with a fascinating collection of farm tools and cow bells found on travels to Nepal, Africa, and Japan, below. Two iron vases shaped like a flowerpot and watering can direct attention to the garden outside.

The fluidity of the natural room's arrangement finds its parallel in nature's individual elements, whether outdoors or brought inside. When we look at forms and surfaces in nature, we see the visible manifestation of a moment in the cycle of growth and decay—an ongoing, living process rather than a completed event. Leaves will eventually fall to the ground and nourish the soil. Even seemingly changeless forms represent moments in time: today's rocks are tomorrow's sand.

Perfection Reconsidered

The poignant "incompleteness" of natural form has been valued as an aesthetic principle in Japanese garden design since ancient times. In such an aesthetic, zig-zag, crooked, or broken lines are considered more beautiful than straight, complete, and perfect lines, and groupings of odd numbers (suggesting incompleteness) are preferred to those of even numbers—directly contradicting the hard-edged, streamlined aesthetic of symmetry so central to Western culture. Instead of the straight, clean lines produced in the finishing of chrome, molded plastics, or even planed and polished wood, nature presents the knobbly edges of rough bark, the twisting and unpredictable lines of sticks, twigs, branches, grasses—whether they're propped in a corner of the room or bent into furnishings or baskets. The more "unfinished" the material the more it exhibits the growth process. A log table, for example, or a chandelier fashioned from tree roots, retains the complex visual reality of nature. Set against the clear geometry and pared-down decor of the contemporary room, such visual richness stands out in bold relief.

Nature contains its own order or design, one radically different from the logically determined order imposed by the rational mind. Because it has come about through evolutionary processes, it is in some sense design "correct" or "perfect," even though it does not conform to any of our established theories about symmetry, balance, or clarity of line. Even where symmetry does occur, as in some shells and flowers, it contains a rhythm far more complex and visually compelling than exists in most human design because it is achieved so effortlessly.

In many respects, the process of form-making in nature finds its parallel in vernacular design. Like trees or seashells, the forms of utilitarian objects and structures—such as sheds, barns, rakes, pitchforks, and other tools—evolve over time, gradually reaching perfection as successive generations seek to make them better in terms of usefulness and economy of production. There is nothing self-conscious or contrived in their appearance. They are designed and re-designed to serve a specific function, to survive wear and tear, to fit the hand or the land as well as possible. They are, in other words, design perfect, which may be one reason why a display of scythes hung on the wall or an old watering can brought indoors and holding masses of fresh daffodils can be so pleasing to the eye.

Increasingly, such examples of vernacular design—particularly those many artifacts of wood and iron associated with garden or farm life, such as wheelbarrows or even old ox yokes—are being used decoratively, not only by those creating a country look, but also in a variety of settings as visual antidotes to the rush of designer objects currently on the market.

In a Tennessee home, dried golden celosia adds color to a weathered wood wall, beneath a Mexican tin outdoor-indoor candle holder, above. A window box filled with dried flowers is an ingenious touch in an urban kitchen, below.

The Colors of Nature

Evoking the outdoors can be as simple as bringing some elements from nature indoors—a basket of vines, a huge, eroded rock, a bunch of pussy willows whose buds unfold, day by day. It can also be a matter of palette: although all colors exist in nature, there is a special quality to them and to their organization. The most prevalent tones are the neutrals and muted hues: browns, beiges, grays, creamy yellows, burnt oranges, and green (which the Japanese see as the center of the spectrum and the most balanced of neutral colors). These are the "ground" against which the brights of flowers, berries, and vivid minerals stand out. Increasingly, this balance of neutral and bright is being brought indoors, most successfully when wood, straw, plaster, cotton, and other natural materials are left untreated. The

serenity of the traditional Japanese home, for instance, is achieved largely through the use of light green or yellow straw, dark wood, white mulberry paper, bark, and bamboo, together with the dark, restful green of plants. Alternatively, the pigments (and their mediums) used to give color to the home—whether in wall paints, furnishing fabrics, or floor rugs—might be derived from nature.

A list of the dyeing agents found in the wild reads like a catalogue of the vegetable and mineral world: among them specific petals, stems, stigmas, berries, fruits, barks, roots, nuts, seeds, shells, rocks, insects, and metallic salts of the earth. The hues most commonly produced from these sources are muted yellows, reds, browns, grays, and blues: a warm, harmonious palette. Naturally dyed

Serene, golden-toned wood walls contrast with a brightly hued South American rug, above. The same colors are picked up in a fragrant display of dried flowers, grasses, seedheads, and mosses on the table. The colors in this California dining room, opposite, have been chosen to harmonize with garden views. The hues of plants and flowers, indoors and out, are set against muted blues and pinks, the mottled, yellow-washed wall, and the sun-faded colors of the Indonesian batik window shades.

fabrics and yarns have a gentleness of tone that softens with
time and exposure to sunlight
but never loses its depth.

The re-introduction of natural
pigments in paints and finishes
began in the '80s, as designers
searched for eloquent treatments
that could breathe some life into
the flat, soulless surfaces of wallboard and other factory finishes.
With the advent of the Green
movement (and spurred by recent recognition of the potential
for ill side-effects of chemically
based pigments and bases), organic paints and dyes using
vegetal and mineral matter have
become available commercially.

Some designers are applying
natural pigments to fresh plaster
as the Minoans did in painting
their frescoes, creating highly
modulated effects reminiscent of
surfaces in nature. Others are
using the translucency of color
washes—typically, natural
dyes in a casein and beeswax
medium—in several layers to
create worlds of living color
with the iridescence of pearl.
Color washes allow the grain
and texture of natural materials
to show through; other natural
finishes might be applied in a
way that gives a crackly, sun-
and wind-beaten look.

In a New York apartment, above, the colors of materials weathered by sun, wind, and rain take on
a bleached look or, in the case of the watering can, a patina that clearly recalls the outdoors.

Surprise Encounters

A collection of wire egg baskets, above, proves very versatile in a Southwest home. They can be paired with wire garden furniture for a light and airy feel, or displayed for their sculptural beauty, as shown here.

Evoking the outdoors in the home can also mean examining the way in which the natural environment impacts on our visual sense. As we move through the untamed world outside, we experience it most potently as a series of surprise encounters. A lightning-struck tree looms suddenly from a green field. A sumptuous flower offers a brief splash of color. Soft, feathery weeds erupt from the crevices between jagged rocks.

There are various forms of expression for this element of surprise when the outdoors is brought inside—a glimpse of delicately colored birds' eggs nestled in a rough straw basket; the odd pinecone still attached to the wood of a kitchen chair. Elsewhere, the element of surprise might be rooted in contrast. The renowned decorator Mark Hampton describes the mill outside Paris where the Duke and Duchess of Windsor would spend their weekends and summers. In a large, elegant room furnished with English and French antiques, a room graced by tall windows and highly polished floors, stood two rugged tree stumps, a large clay pot of geraniums on each. In other rooms, rather than sur-

Pots of geraniums, gardening boots, and a hat, below, define this as a transitional space between the indoors and the outdoors. In a particularly unusual act of recycling, the owners converted a First World War gunpowder barrel into an innovative umbrella stand.

Utilitarian objects associated with farm life decorate this Rhode Island living room, right. A collection of peculiarly shaped sea shells and a lobster pot serving as a plant table establish a sense of place and recall the presence of nearby beaches.

prising through contrast, nature astonishes the beholder with its elegantly restrained beauty. A tracery of twigs against the stratified gray of a slate table evokes the stark yet exhilarating clarity of winter scenes.

Chaos and cohesion combine in the natural world. Visual scenes evolve, season by season and year by year, without regard for the eye of the beholder. Living things sprout and flourish wherever conditions permit, never in elegant, studied locations; weeds take hold and spread, engulfing large areas; moss creeps over stone, wood, and earth. Yet nothing clashes, nothing seems out of place. Even as it ages and decays, nature continues to be visually attractive. The sea grass that grows straight and green on the margins of a sandy beach still delights the eye after it turns to brown and is twisted into dry clumps.

In this sense, nature provides the perfect model for a certain kind of stylistic informality that melds with ease of living. The link between nature brought indoors and a more relaxed lifestyle has its origins in the Georgian interiors of the early nineteenth century, when wigs, denoting artifice, were removed,

when potted plants and cut flowers began to populate drawing rooms, along with the low coffee table that is now taken for granted as a focus for easy sociability. At the time, letting one's hair down (literally) and inviting the outside in were virtually synonymous ideas.

Today, organic order is echoed in an intuitive and flexible interior style, one that yields to impulse. Wildflowers, with their disordered yet always compatible craze of colors, are brought inside and stood, in no particular arrangement, in a milk pail, an iron garden urn, a pitcher. Fascinating river pebbles, oddly shaped seedpods, large, sculptural fungi, or pieces of bark are gathered as they attract the eye, to be displayed decoratively as treasures that have a personal value, if not a material one.

During the Mannerist period throughout Europe, following the Renaissance, noblemen assembled rooms filled with all manner of natural and scientific articles: skulls, armillary spheres, chambered nautilus shells, and other pseudoscientific odds and ends were intermingled in cabinet tableaux. Similarly, at the time of the Sung Dynasty in China (960–1280), certain natural objects were considered virtually priceless. Emissaries were sent out from the court to search far and wide for magnificently eroded rocks that were sent back, along with exotic flowers, in "flower-and-rock caravans," to be displayed on pedestals or used for vines to climb up, in imitation of vine-festooned cliffs.

Furnishings made from weathered elemental materials—from cane, straw, twigs, or iron, for instance—can be just as impressive as gilded and carved period pieces. At the same time, they carry the suggestion of relaxed living, as does a decorative use of the materials themselves. Just as a column of slender branches or a stack of straw cannot help but soften a highly structured setting, so an old wicker chair, or a table made from a slab of rough stone, sets the tone for a kind of shirtsleeve, even barefoot informality. These are the kinds of much loved furnishings that, under the dictates of high style, were previously relegated to the only setting that seemed fitting—the garden, the porch, or maybe the summer house. Today, with high style adopting a more natural emphasis, they have a place indoors, whatever the season.

House as Garden

Wicker chairs and ash tables add to the light feeling of this conservatory in the West country of England, above.

In a more formal setting, the introduction of nature untamed gives the formality an edge, throws it off balance as a willow tree blown almost horizontal by the wind modifies the tone of a garden of carefully clipped topiary and shaped beds. Many of today's leading floral designers are showing how effectively the simple, untamed elements of nature can be superimposed on the highly cultivated to create a stunning counterpoint.

Of course, a room is not like the wild, where nature grows untamed by human touch or thought. The home environment can be most closely compared to the garden—a place that represents the marriage of natural process and the human hand, with chance and will playing equal roles. But this is not the only reason the garden has become the most pervasive force behind the natural style interior. The garden provides inspiration in the creation of the home environment because it symbolizes, historically, so many of the enduring qualities of life that, in contrast to the opulent materialism of the '80s, are becoming primary values in many people's lives today. As Thomas Mawson, a turn-of-the-century nurseryman, wrote, it is our object in the garden to escape "the hard, materialistic, common, literal facts of daily life."

Devoted through much of its history to production rather than to consumption, the garden—whether indoor or outdoor—is a potent symbol of our links with the earth and the creativity that we share with it. Given this, it should come as no surprise that the French couturier Hubert de Givenchy has said that he prefers to sketch not in any of the grand rooms of his sixteenth-century chateau, but in his simple, domed, garden pavilion, filled as it is with gardening tools, gloves, flower seeds, and mementos from trips to the gardens

he loves in various parts of the world.

The garden, since Eden, has represented the ideal. It is paradise not only in the Judeo-Christian cosmos but in many others too. The concept of the garden as sanctuary, filled with peace and growth, has existed throughout history, and throughout history cartographers have placed this idealized garden somewhere on their maps of the known world—where hardly matters.

The idea of the garden, like the idea of home, also denotes security and refuge. In Hebrew the word *gan*, "garden," is related to the term "to defend" or "shelter," while the old English word from which our own *garden* is derived means "enclosure" or "dwelling," making the garden a perfect metaphor for the home. Early gardens were indeed like small, ordered, outdoor rooms, walled against the wild lands that were a constant source of anxiety.

Mediterranean gardens and courtyards are still walled, serving as all-purpose, sensual transitions between the outside and the inside. Because the climate does not encourage the kind of year-round flower gardening possible in England, architectural ornament has al-

A London floral designer decorated an antique samovar with an arrangement of dried red roses and pine cones; just about any intriguing-looking object —whether old or contemporary—becomes even more visually striking when grouped with carefully selected natural elements.

ways been more widely used here, with plaques, fountains, statues, and seating all playing a part. Bushy, Mediterranean herbs such as bay and rosemary, and small trees—orange and lemon trees especially—are grown in containers rather than in beds, and moved into prominent positions as they flower. There are even specially designed pots on wheels that allow for instant repositioning of plants— and also make it easy to roll small trees onto the terrace for a direct dose of sunlight. This type of garden has served as a model for several interiors today that feature simple wood or iron garden furniture, stone floors, and terra-cotta plantings of herbs and flowers.

There are other models, too, offering visual inspiration for the natural style interior. The cozy, domestic garden of Victorian England, with its abundance of flowers and foliage in irregular groupings and its light wicker or cane, has provided inspiration for many a light-filled conservatory. The cottage garden, where herbs, roses, and marigolds are grown for future use, has been reinterpreted in a French interior that features dried roses gathered into arrangements evocative of the sculptured hedges of French

cottage gardens, tied with raffia, and held in wicker baskets surrounded by Provençal prints and faience. The unstructured sprawl of the "wilderness" garden that became popular in the eighteenth century along with twig furniture and verdant moss and all things rustic—a refuge not from the unfathomable land beyond, but from the highly cultivated society of the day—is also inspiring the design and decoration of many of today's homes.

Those rooted in a more minimal aesthetic might take for inspiration the Eastern garden. Built on restraint mixed with a genuine delight in nature, traditional gardens in China and Japan are like microcosms of the great, rugged outdoors. Eroded and oddly shaped rocks are placed at intervals to represent mountains; twisted branches take the place of trees; seas or lakes are represented by small pools of water or by tiny streams, which in turn may be symbolized, in the Zen garden, by areas of sand or gravel raked into ripples.

The Japanese garden especially, and the interior inspired by it, is characterized by an austerity offset by the softness of natural forms. This is a highly abstract art form that relies on the creation of an essential order

so that nature itself—the play of sunlight, the movement of the wind, the growth and decay of living things—can be free to do the rest. It is an art of contradictions. The placement of individual elements is carefully planned so that the effect of the whole can seem as uncontrived as in nature. "White areas" of pure space encourage the eye to rest and contemplate, in their absence, nature's powerful presences.

The New York–based designer Clodagh creates carefully restrained yet natural interiors that are in many ways analogous to the Japanese garden. Just as the gardener in Japan trains a young tree to bend as it would with age, never forcing it against its inherent character, Clodagh rusts sheets of metal with acids and uses them to construct fixtures. Water, one of nature's elemental forces, cascades across pebbles in a water sculpture. There is nothing superfluous; whatever is there serves to satisfy many senses at once, leaving empty spaces so the eye can rest.

One of the aims of classical Chinese garden design is to "make the small evoke the large" by borrowing visual motifs from natural scenery. The ordering process of human endeavor is

In a New York interior designer's loft, opposite, a dramatic display of bare twigs emphasizes the wintry outdoor look created by pale sandblasted brick walls and tall iron candlestands.

A detail of the arrangement, above, shows a cherrywood sand table, equipped with tiny rocks and a rake for producing the kind of textural patterns created by Zen monks in their sand and rock gardens. A small stick of herbal incense positioned on its own holder need only be lit to add the dimension of scent.

thus given a meaning far broader than the cultural statement that any design represents. The same could be said of the present trend toward bringing the outdoors into the home.

There are as many kinds of garden rooms as there are types of garden. In a serenely elegant New York interior, Parisian designers Patrick Naggar and Terese Carpenter created an environment that combines neo-classical style with an Eastern reverence for nature. Regal bird cages stand on specially designed silver-plated bronze supports shaped as tree branches, attached to walls of hand-polished Venetian stucco. In the powder room, a Ruhlmann sconce casts its light on a wall shelf in which fine holes have been drilled to hold strands of ornamental grass, or a single flower brought back from

The uneven lines of unplaned wood dominate in this log house, left, creating an easy transition to the woodland outside the window. In this natural-style home, plants and furniture are of equal visual and decorative significance.

a country house. In the living room, textured rush matting, evoking moist riverbanks, melds gracefully with eighteenth century armchairs.

For suburban and rural homes, an ideal way to bring the outside in is by capitalizing on the view of the world just outside the window. In a rural area outside of Atlanta, Georgia, one couple created a treehouse effect by building the many-windowed addition to their house high among the treetops. And in Minnesota, a family planted a textured garden of specimen trees, flowers, and small foliage plants just outside the floor-to-ceiling windows running the length of their ranch-style home. From inside, the effect, with birds and butterflies constantly darting about, is not unlike that of an aquarium.

This unusual rustic chandelier and chair—reminiscent of the furnishings of Victorian country lodges—were created by a furniture maker for a house in upstate New York, right. The chandelier is crafted entirely from tree roots. Tree stumps form a base for a glass table top below.

Inspiration for the home comes from the all-American porch, evocative of long, hot summers. However grand the architectural style of the house, these summer living spaces are designed for relaxed lounging, with their peeling rocking chairs, wicker sofas, swings, palm-leaf fans, iced tea, and plants arranged haphazardly on old planks. Outdoor furnishings might be given cohesion by a single paint color, typically "shutter" green or white. Or the wood might be left unpainted to weather to silver gray.

Endless Summer

There is a timeless quality to many of the rooms created in the natural style. It is the timelessness that comes from perpetual adaptation and change, characteristic of all things that are part of nature.

Whether it evokes the ruggedness of the wild, the gentleness of the garden, or the relaxed ease of porch or courtyard, the outdoor-infused interior reflects a desire for more enduring values in our lives: for homes in which, as Frank Lloyd Wright once put it, we may "take root and grow."

The architect of this Fifties house located in Devon, England, removed part of the exterior wall and added a conservatory to form an indoor porch, opposite.

The classical Mediterranean courtyard is one of the earliest architectural devices for creating a connection between house and garden. In this Southern California courtyard adaptation, above, glass doors in the home lead to a flower-filled balcony overlooking an herb and vegetable bed.

Chapter Two

THE TOUCH OF THE OUTDOORS

*Touch is the parent of our eyes, ears, nose,
and mouth. It is the sense which became
differentiated into the others, a fact that seems
to be recognized in the age-old evaluation of touch as
"the mother of the senses."*

—ASHLEY MONTAGUE, *TOUCHING:
THE HUMAN SIGNIFICANCE OF SKIN*

When an American critic, writing about the 1930 International Exposition of Decorative Arts in Paris, described the new style we now call Art Deco as being "not for the lover of maple and pine, not for the partisan of cotton and horsehair," he drew attention to a search for sophistication that meant abandoning the materials of the past. In the same exposition, the public had its first view of Le Corbusier's vision for the future of domestic architecture—the unornamented house in which every form, every surface, was as smooth and clean as the steel from which the physical world of the late twentieth century was to be constructed.

Soon wallboard, plastics, and other highly processed materials were to divorce us even further from the tactile experiences that had once been provided by wood, plaster, iron, clay, reed, wool, stone—natural materials from the outdoor world. Only now, with the issues of ecology, personal health, comfort, and spiritual well-being coming to the forefront, are these materials from nature being brought back indoors, and with them a complex world of form and texture unseen in home design for some time.

For some, it is a yearning for rich texture itself that has inspired an outdoor look in the home. One designer, for instance, unable to live comfortably with the bland surfaces of her apartment walls and floors, dismantled an old barn and used the rough barn wood to create a highly textured new "skin" inside her living space. The new surfaces, with their aura of rusticity, help to transform an anonymous, urban interior into an environment that feels pleasurable.

The sense of touch relates directly to the quality of life. It's a relationship built into our language—*to feel* means both to perceive through touch and to experience an emotion or state of health. Nearly everyone has, at one time or another, felt a wave of relaxation and pleasure on handling a rock smoothed by water, or on running the fingers through a luxuriously soft patch of grass.

We are born into the world with a highly developed sense of touch, and our earliest experiences are tactile. Unable to focus our vision at any distance, we simply perceive through the sense receptors beneath our skin, gradually giving meaning to those perceptions.

A contemporary urban apartment, previous page, was transformed into a textural feast, using weathered wood. Beach grass, above, can be woven into baskets. In the study of a cottage in the English Lake District, stacks of baskets and wheat draw the eye upward, opposite.

Surface and Sensibility

This conservatory room in Gloucestershire, England, as well as the rustic barrel table and plank chairs, were crafted entirely from salvaged woods. Here the boundary between outside and inside virtually disappears. The tall, woven forms pictured on the left are fishermen's skeps.

Some things feel comfortingly soft and warm to the touch. Others feel hard, cold, sharp, or rough. Soon, as the visual system matures, and the infant comes into contact with a wider environment, it begins to seek out the feel of things in order to learn about the relationship between touch and sight. It is through the skin that we learn about the textures and forms of our immediate environment, and even as adults, it is by touching that we confirm what we see, a fact represented in an old phrase that has fallen into disuse in our visually oriented world—"true to touch."

Touch is not only the first sense to develop—both in human development and in human evolution—it is also the most diffuse of all our senses. Yet the more we focus our attention on the visual qualities of our environment, and the more we inhabit environments designed to please our visual sense alone, the less we are able to appreciate those subtler tactile qualities. Students at the Bauhaus had to be taught to gauge texture and to form an understanding of materials not by sight but by touch. Encouraged to learn about the smoothness or coarseness of materials by feeling the surfaces with their fingers, the students discovered, for instance, that untreated wood is soft, while polished wood is hard; that steel is cold, while clay is warm.

This aspect of the Bauhaus teaching philosophy was based on a belief that highly civilized Western people have lost their sensitivity to textural qualities—a sensitivity central to the experiences not only of children but of less civilized peoples too. Perhaps we have lost this sensitivity because mass production techniques and synthetic materials tend to produce a uniformity in surface and form that do nothing to stimulate our sense of touch. If the hand is, as the philosopher Immanuel Kant once stated, the body's "outer brain," then our outer brains risk being deadened by the environments in which we spend so much of our time.

The natural world, by comparison, is rich in its diversity of contrasting textures and forms: soft moss on hard rock, conifer branches encrusted with lichens, smooth leaves against rough bark, broken shells on sand. Cattails, honesty, pussy willow, and many of the forty-five hundred species of grasses that grow in the wild attract us not so much for color but rather for textures.

In a Manhattan loft, soft, shaggy grass grows in Italian terra-cotta planters on each window ledge, while a Fifties picnic cooler serves as a plant table, below. A wooden cow brings the feel of the barnyard into the city and completes the outdoor scene.

One New York designer enjoys waking up and imagining himself in a bosquelike setting, left overleaf. In his city home, ivy tumbles from an urn atop a pedestal on a grass "rug." In an alcove, right overleaf, he offsets a cool, neoclassical style with outdoor textures, lining a shelf with rye grass that he waters daily.

For tactile qualities alone, a look at the homes of indigenous peoples in various parts of the world can be a revelation in the textural beauty of materials from nature brought indoors—the decorated bark cloth, for instance, that covers the interior walls of the typical South Pacific dwelling; the crushed coral floors of Samoan homes; or the tangle of twisting branches that forms the ceiling of a Mauritanian interior, with its softly molded earth walls, palmwood sitting platforms, and grass mats.

Frank Lloyd Wright's "organic architecture," as he called it, is notable for its use of natural textures and forms that echo those of the sites on which he built. The interior of a house on Long Island, New York, for instance, is defined by cypress boards and battens. At Taliesen West in Arizona, Wright used reinforced concrete but poured it around locally found rocks. Combined with this rock embedded "desert concrete," as he called it, the rough, redwood beams and cotton canvas roof of Taliesen create interiors that seem to flow from the vast desert landscape outside.

The Textured Home

Instead of sculpture, Wright used large rocks that had been inscribed, centuries earlier, by Native Americans.

Wright was influenced in his use of materials by Japanese architecture. All the materials used to construct, furnish, and decorate the traditional Japanese home are pleasant to touch and harmonious with the land. Straw tatami mats covering the floors feel warm and silky to bare feet (although we usually think of the hands as being the most receptive to touch, the feet, too, are highly sensitive). At the same time, when trod on, they emit a warm, sweet aroma. Interior walls, or *shoji* screens, are made from soft, almost downy mulberry paper. Posts of wood, often with the bark retained, recall the textures of trunks and branches—roofs are sometimes supported by branches, some still sprouting leaves. Even in the contemporary Japanese interior, great attention is paid to tactile qualities. Wallboard is often covered in cloth, and interior walls of exposed concrete are given the rough, textural quality of nature's own materials.

In an Arizona artist's residence, South American clay jugs, rough plaster, and wood, opposite above, suggest the tactile experiences found outdoors. Dried grasses offer a wealth of textures, opposite below, and can easily be anchored in place with small stones in a pottery vase.

A wall lined with rough stones hauled from a dry local riverbed and a ceiling of wooden boards braced with forest logs transform a contemporary house near Toronto, above. The color-washed sheetrock wall was textured with sand. Visual and tactile appeal are equally important rustic furniture design. A dining table with contrasting wood inlay, right, displays both qualities.

Traditional dwellings, by necessity, use materials that are easily attainable from the surrounding land—which is what makes the interiors seem so happily at home in their wider environments. In these houses, the outdoors and indoors flow naturally into each other because

clay define the character of the desert home, both the Southwestern adobe house in the United States and the tower houses of Yemen. We associate the tropical interior with the silky-smooth textures of rattan, cane, and bamboo, offset by coarse coir matting made from

there is a continuity of texture and form between the two. Local woods from nearby trees form the essence of the typical mountain dwelling—the Adirondack cabin, for instance, with its robust log furniture and pinecones in the fireplace. The softly undulating forms of sun-baked

the husk of the coconut palm fruit. Rushes, reeds, and straw, whether woven or bundled into sheaves for thatching, and timber evoke the old English dwelling, while the traditional Mediterranean interior is characterized by heavy wood, cool stone, and clay.

E a r t h l y   G o o d s

Why do the highly tactile qualities possessed by these minimally processed, natural materials tend to evoke comfort? When Bauhaus teachers Marcel Breuer and Mies Van der Rohe wanted to make more comfortable chairs, they used woods and grasses. Breuer's side chair was designed to be made from wood and woven rattan. Reminiscent of seventeenth-century furniture design, the tubular frame of Van der Rohe's Weissenhof chair was covered in handwoven cane. Similarly, when Ralph Lauren offers his "basket-weave" print sheets as part of his empire of designer comfort, he is playing on our tendency to associate natural and familiar textures with satisfying tactile experiences.

Perhaps natural materials appeal to our sense of touch because they tend to be inherently "soft." Even rock, among the hardest of natural materials, can nevertheless have soft curves if it has been brought from a riverbank where the water has gradually smoothed away its sharp edges. Elemental metals, which come directly from the earth, also have soft qualities. Unlike hard alloys such as steel (a word that comes from the Danish *staal*, or "ice"), the "natural" metals are soft enough to be

workable by hand. Iron, for instance, has been worked since as far back as 4000 B.C., long before the people of the Iron Age started to make tools with it. Like other elemental metals, including copper and tin, iron is a "warm" metal because of its coarse surface texture.

Architectural historian Steen Rasmussen believes that we identify rounded forms as soft because they make us think of those pliable materials that can be bent, kneaded, twisted, or molded by the fingers into such inviting shapes. Clay, for instance, produced by nature from particles of rock mixed with water, is a highly workable substance that in its final, baked form retains its suggestion of softness and malleability. Could this be why in so many creation myths god is said to have made humans from clay?

There is an inherent affinity between our own bodies and the living things of the outdoor world that provide materials for our use. We speak of a person's limbs like tree limbs, and of skin as soft as rose petals. We compare our bones to sticks— whether green and pliable or old and brittle—and hard muscle to rock, or to iron. We identify with the materials of the natural world because, physically, we have so much in common with them. We too, after all, are creatures of nature. And so, just as we like to touch another body with our own, we are attracted to the feel of materials brought in from the outdoors.

We feel attracted to objects made by hand from the materials of nature, not only for their softness, but also perhaps because we sense the touch of another person in their making. There is something about the slightly irregular feel of a bowl turned or coiled by hand, for instance, that makes it comfortable to touch and hold. The natural style interior derives its character from the very imperfections in form and finish that are so often a part of simple hand processes, just as they are a part of nature. Whereas in the recent past we learned to look for synthetic finishes and the perfect smoothness that denotes quality in factory-produced objects (and that tend to diminish with age and wear), today it is the inherent quirks of a more natural style—the knots in pine, the stains made by mineral deposits in marble, the odd twists and turns in a twig chair, or the imperfect roundness of an iron chair leg—that lend to the home its atmosphere of ease.

In a Manhattan apartment spiky twigs contrast with the smooth ripples of a table top made from a slab of purple stone, opposite above. The stone was brought from upstate New York.

A straw-shaded floor lamp illuminates a quiet corner in the conservatory of a Cotswold stone cottage, opposite below. Instead of traditional grout, moss was used to finish the tiled floor in this garden pavilion, above.

The visual qualities of natural materials tell us a great deal about how they feel, giving us vivid impressions of hard and soft, heavy and light, warm or cold, smooth or coarse. We make what has been called "imaginative physical contact" with the objects in our visual world that we once touched. We can see how they feel, even without touching, and the way we perceive them is informed, quite often, by our past association with nature—making the materials from the outdoors all the more evocative.

We remember the feeling of spiky grass or soft moss underfoot, of ferns brushing against our legs or leaves against our face. Through the soles of our shoes, we know how it would feel to walk on silky rush or granular stone with bare feet. A bundle of soft grasses invites us to touch because, just by looking, we know that to touch those leaves would feel pleasurably soft and feathery. Even if in our daily lives we are denied the experience of sifting sand through our fingers or of peeling bark from a twig, we can evoke those experiences for ourselves visually through the materials with which we surround ourselves in our homes.

Out of the Woods

THE TOUCH OF THE OUTDOORS

A daybed of soft-to-the-touch, un-peeled birch logs, a bark basket filled with feathery dried grasses, a wool blanket and pillow, and a knob-bly, bark-covered pitcher and cups set impart warmth to the guest room in a seaside home, opposite. A bird cage with a twig roof sits in the natural-style parlor, below.

In a Connecticut den, right, above and below, a classic office chair is warmed by a textural twist of nature. The unusual table was re-cycled from pieces of warped beech-wood accented by an ebony inlay. Wood salvaged from a granary was used to timber the ceiling.

The artless beauty of wood in its natural state is being appreciated anew. Recently, there has been a revival in the use of natural treat-ments, such as beeswax, which give woods a soft luster without detracting from their softness or the decorative qualities of their grain. Each kind of wood has its own textural qualities. Ash and hickory, used extensively for farm tools, have a strong, coarse texture. Maple has a very deco-rative, wavy grain that lends itself to furniture making. Pear wood, with its fine texture, is easily turned and is therefore used for bowls and other uten-sils. Oak, a frequent choice for outdoor use because of its dura-bility, has a beautiful "silver grain." The most tantalizing grains are found in woods from the thickest, oldest trees—those very trees that have almost dis-appeared from our landscapes.

The qualities of these woods are emphasized when they are weathered by being exposed to the elements.

Like all natural materials, wood ages beautifully—as any-one knows who has found a piece of silvery driftwood, its pith worn away and its grain standing out in relief. Similarly, furniture left out on the porch to be beaten by sun, rain, and wind

gains a special character and soothing touch.

Because many of the hardwoods once preferred for outdoor furniture, such as mahogany and teak, are endangered, the more sustainable softwoods are gaining in popularity among those who wish to preserve nature. Where endangered woods are used, they are increasingly being bought from managed sources; many furniture makers are recycling woods both for the sake of preservation and for the quality of the grain that the old, majestic trees offered. Others prefer to use native woods as a way of retaining the link with what's outside the door. There is a strong movement among designers toward the use of rough-hewn, unfinished woods normally associated with rustic pieces or picnic furniture. Branches, logs, and twigs are being brought indoors and bent, woven, or nailed, occasionally with bark still intact and pinecones attached. Straight willow branches are used as curtain rails or, as in the garden, are bent into arches, trained with ivy, and used as room dividers. Tree stumps support tabletops (as with the imaginative and innovative work of Los Angeles designer Brian Murphy).

A mirror frame made from a hollow cross-section of a tree stump imparts an imaginative, fairy-tale touch to a British living room. Some of the most satisfyingly textural objects are borrowed from birds. Above, an abandoned nest is filled with smooth eggs and silky swallows' feathers, making it appear inhabited.

Other materials, too, are being used "in the raw" as a way of bringing the textural outdoor world indoors and creating an environment in which human intervention in nature is kept to a minimum. Marble, normally polished so highly that it looks light and insubstantial, may now be broken and only lightly polished so that its ragged edges show it for what it is—a hard, nonporous stone that belongs to the earth. Plaster, made from slaked lime and coarse sand mixed with water (once upon a time, chopped straw or feathers helped bind the mixture), is left unpainted for its naturally cream or pink tones, or may be rubbed with earth pigments to preserve its porous, chalky texture. Cotton, linen, and wool are left unbleached and untreated. Strips of bark are woven into baskets or chair seats, while bamboo is simply split for use as wall coverings or window shades, used whole for framing furniture (bamboo is thus the "warm" precursor of tubular stainless steel), or woven into mats.

When woven, fibers such as bark, bamboo, reeds, rushes, and jute produce some of the most texturally alive surfaces. In fact, the word *texture* itself comes from the verb *to weave*, and

Crafting with Nature

The word *texture* comes from the verb "to weave," and every weaving has its own tactile quality. In an Illinois farmhouse, above, a tightly woven wool rug hangs behind a chair of smooth, woven wicker and bent bamboo. On the chair, a leafy potpourri is kept in a basket roughly woven from twigs and moss. Dried hydrangea in the pail add crinkly texture.

originally meant a textile, whose texture was determined by the kind of threads used and the manner of their arrangement. Baskets and mats, even hammocks, are woven in many different ways and from many different materials—depending on the region from which they originate and the folk tradition in which they are made. Sisal matting, for example, woven from fibers extracted from the leaves of the Mexican agave cactus, has a tough, naturally cool feel. Coir produces a coarse matting. Basket making is one of the oldest crafts known to humankind (and to birds, who weave their nests with twigs and grasses).

Baskets of all types are woven from materials found right outside the door: in Africa, from savannah grasses; in England, from the twigs of willow, especially from the species known as 'Velvet osier.' In South Carolina, sweet grass found in seaside marshes was long ago adopted for basket weaving by African slaves, who had perfected their craft over generations using savannah grasses. The pliant fibers are traditionally coiled and "stitched." Southern designer Randy Outz has even found a new use for the ubiquitous kudzu vine: He bends the ten-

drils into natural birdhouses, which look as beautiful inside the home as in the yard.

While baskets, created for utilitarian rather than decorative ends, are generally woven from one or two elements, decorative wreaths may be woven from a combination of widely different materials—including dry grasses, branches, vines, and twigs—twisted into circlets, and laced with dried or fresh flowers, herbs, leaves, moss, seedpods, feathers, and even fungi. As such, wreaths, textural microcosms of the outside world, celebrate nature's riches.

Like a wreath, the natural style interior creates an outdoor feel—in the true sense of the word—by weaving together a blend of materials. The texture may be woven from diverse strands to create a wider, eclectic "landscape." A collection of sculptural gourds, an iron bench and moss-covered terra-cotta pots overflowing with ivy from the garden, a wall finished in smooth stones brought from a riverbank, a display of baskets woven from grasses that grow as far apart as North Carolina, England, and Africa—all or some of these elements can help to make of indoor life a richly sensuous experience.

Coiled willow—used to make wicker—is displayed alongside a collection of baskets woven from different materials, complete with leaves and pine cones, above. Simple and inexpensive accessories such as these can convert an ordinary room into a natural paradise and go a long way in bringing the outside inside.

Chapter Three

THE SCENT
OF THE
OUTDOORS

And because the breath of flowers is far sweeter in the Air (where it comes and goes, like the Warbling of Musick) than in the hand, therefore nothing is more fit for that delight, than to know what be the flowers and plants that do best perfume the Air.

—FRANCIS BACON, ''OF GARDENS''

You sit in your garden, admiring the canvas of color composed by flowers and grass, feeling the refreshing breeze as it brushes your skin, listening to the birds. You take a walk through the fall woods, stooping to gather an armful of crispy brown leaves and craning your neck for a glimpse of a bird's nest. And all the time that you are looking and touching and listening, your senses are bombarded by scents of which you are barely conscious yet that will live on deep in the recesses of your memory.

How much of our experience of nature is conveyed by scent! In the early days of March and April, when the fresh, young smells of apple blossom, daffodil, and hyacinth hang in the air, we speak of the "rebirth of earth" and the delicious sensation of "spring fever." The pleasures of the garden would not be the same without the scented flowers—the honey-like early bulbs, crocus and iris, the cowslips and lilac of May, the peonies and roses of summer. Yet, even though we associate these sweet smells with warm, garden days, most gardens in our time are not nearly as heavily scented as they once were—and, despite bunches of cut flowers brought indoors, neither are our houses fragranced with nature.

Ever since the 1600s, when gardeners began to give precedence to the look of flowers, we have been the victims of what, earlier in this century, Ruth Beebe Wilder in *The Fragrant Garden* called, "the long tyranny of the greedy sense over the less assertive one, the triumph of the eye over the nose." Even in early nineteenth-century England there existed over two hundred varieties of scented geranium, with lemonish-smelling leaves, and leaves that smelled spicy, minty, or rose-like. They were grown for use in rose perfumes and potpourris, but were soon overtaken by flowering geraniums and relegated to farm kitchens and greenhouses. Marigolds, too, were cultivated profusely for their scent, and having been harvested were kept dried in sacks and shaped into fragrant nosegays and garlands that would see the family through the bleak winter months. A true connoisseur of scent in nature, Wilder—who penned her essays refreshed by the sweet-smelling nosegay that sat on her writing table—wrote of bringing a branch of witch hazel indoors in February to fill the air of a warm room with fragrance.

Nevertheless, for all her skill in identifying the scents of nature, Wilder struggled to describe what her "receptive nose" experienced.

A conservatory, previous page, has been turned into an indoor herb garden. Eucalyptus naturally scents a room, above. Household objects, dried flowers, and flourishing plants form a charming, romantic melange.

Scent Through the Centuries

The triumph of the "greedy sense" over the more subtle sense of smell has left us with a vocabulary ill equipped to express the wealth of scents existing in the natural world, especially as compared to the rich vocabulary that exists for color. *Sweet* is the word most often used. But many of the most pleasant natural scents are deliciously unsweet. Take, for instance, the sharp, lemony scent of mock oranges, or the spicy, almost pungent smell of American bayberries.

Among roses alone, there exists a wide range of markedly different scents—which makes "roses" and "scent" almost interchangeable ideas. The ancient damask rose, with its magenta pigment, is the most heady. Some, such as 'Peer Gynt,' are spicy. Some varieties have a sharp scent; others suffuse the air with apple-y or lemony aromas, while the musk rose is known for its nostalgic, musty aroma.

Flower scents tend to force themselves upon one, demanding attention and occasionally leaving us jaded. Leaf smells, usually from the aromatic herbs or "nose-herbs," as Shakespeare called them, are subtler, and many leaves only give off their scent secretively when touched or approached: this is true of rosemary, bay, sweetfern, juniper, thyme, southernwood, and most sweet herbs. Perhaps because they are not so free with their scent—often, a leaf must be crushed in order to release its perfume—they hold it longer than flowers, and are often sweeter dried than fresh, which makes them ideal for year-round, indoor use.

In fact, the use of herbs and spices as natural indoor air fresheners and purifiers is as ancient as the use of writing parchment. Thyme, for instance, gets its name from the classical Greek word for "incense." Mint has long been considered a cooling herb; sprigs of it arranged in a jar in the living room cool the heat of a summer day. Rosemary, with its sweet and spicy aroma, is known as an emblem of constancy because of the long-lasting scent of its dried leaves—as Shakespeare wrote, "here's rosemary for remembrance."

In the past, branches of rosemary were placed under the bed to ensure good dreams, or sprigs slipped under a child's pillow to ward off nightmares. Those who follow herbal lore might grow pots of rosemary on a bedroom window ledge, or hang a bunch from the bedposts, for decoration and sweet dreams.

Herbs and flowers are hung to dry in an English farmhouse kitchen, opposite. A large rosemary bush near the door gives off its aroma whenever it is brushed against. Scented bouquets needn't be confined to tabletops. Tiny, dried rose arrangements create a charming vignette on an antique wire garden chair, above.

The first recorded use of fragrant herbs and flowers to scent the home was in ancient Egypt, where each god or goddess was associated with a particular fragrance. Translations of hieroglyphs show that the Egyptians had an extensive vocabulary for scents. The Greeks, influenced by the Egyptians, used spices from the East in their interiors, and the Romans, who valued above all the tangy scent of lemon verbena for use in nosegays, also indulged in spicy aromas.

But it was in medieval Europe, with its lack of modern conveniences, that the art of bringing scents from the garden into the home reached its zenith. In France, city dwellers would sweeten the air in hallways and parlors by strewing the floors with sweet-smelling straw in winter, and with herbs and flowers in summer: sweet marjoram and rosemary were especially popular for this purpose. As visitors and residents walked over these floors, a fragrance would be released and engage the olfactory sense.

In Spain and Portugal, lavender was cast on floors on festival days so that rooms would look and smell special. In England, pine was burned to purify the air, and rose petals were placed in chests to scent linens, which in turn scented the bedrooms in which they were used. Fennel, rosemary, and sweet woodruff were worn as garlands and brought into the homes to create a gardenesque environment.

But for sheer nasal delight, the most popular English strewing herb was meadowsweet, which was used in chambers, halls, and banqueting rooms in the summertime, for the smell was said to make "hearts merrie." Queen Elizabeth I was reputed to have preferred this herb above all others for lining the floors of her private apartments.

Such practical and delightful customs were observed and eagerly embraced by continental Europe. One Dutchman who visited England in the 1500s remarked on the pleasure he experienced in finding parlors festooned with refreshingly sweet herbs, while nosegays with various kinds of fragrant flowers scented bedrooms and privyrooms, cheering him up and delighting all his senses.

In those times, when many herbs were grown in the garden or picked from the wild for culinary and medicinal purposes, the drying shed or kitchen filled with herbs hung from beams.

THE SCENT OF THE OUTDOORS

Even today, we surround ourselves with scents, hoping to derive promised pleasure from them. We might hang "lavender" air fresheners in the bedroom, wash our dishes with "lemon-scented" detergent, buy "rose petal" bathroom tissue and "pine" air spray for the kitchen. But our noses can't be fooled by these synthetic scents. Although they might mask unpleasant odors and add a temporary hint of sweetness to the air, they do not have the power to move us in the way natural scents can.

Today, one American nature lover is known to put sprigs of fresh mint under her rugs so that every step releases a cool, minty scent. Sachets slipped into bed linens, pomanders hung in wardrobes, and boudoir pillows stuffed with such herbs as hops and mugwort are more traditional means of infusing the home with botanical fragrance. These methods are just as valid—and delightful—today as they were in the past.

Natural scents excite both the memory and the imagination, and stimulate a whole range of emotions, often on a subconscious level. The scent of newly mown grass speaks clearly of midsummer days, while the warm aroma of fresh hay reminds us of

Uplifting and Aromatic

An aromatic kitchen arrangement, opposite, incorporates
green-tinged wheat surrounded
by yellow saffron thistle and various dried materials,
rolls, and garlic. An old fashioned
tussie-mussie, above, yields the scents
of vanilla, cinnamon, ginger, and dried roses.

the fall. The smell of real lemon is closely associated with cleanliness—indeed, lemon has proven antiseptic qualities. And for many people the smell of lavender, traditionally used to scent sheets, still evokes the comfort of sweet sleep.

Flower smells have different cultural associations, from the "cottage smell" of sweet william, and the sweet, innocent scent of wild roses, to the decadent, sophisticated fragrance of lily (which in the old days was believed to be unhealthy for indoor use, even resulting in possible death if breathed overnight in the bedroom!).

An age-old belief that recurs from time to time in cultures all across the world is that scent has the power not only to affect the spirit through its associative qualities, but also to influence the health of both mind and body. One medieval herbal mentioned that one need only smell violets in order to feel better. Basil was said to "maketh a man merry and glad," while sweet marjoram could cure those given over to "much sighing." According to a sixteenth-century herbal, rosemary was a youth enhancer—"smell it and it shall keep you youngly." Thyme and mint refresh the spirits.

Essential
Scents

~~~~

Scented candles and artichoke topiaries made from bay leaves decorate a dining table, above.

mint, rose, and myrtle for anointing. The ancient Japanese art of fragrance, or *kohdoh*, is a therapeutic discipline that relies on the smelling of incense. It's also considered likely that the burning of incense in churches was originally designed to alter the mental state of the faithful, leading to feelings of well-being and even to trance-like states—"to rejoyce, to comfort, to quicken and to rouse and to purify our senses," as Montaigne, a French contemporary of Shakespeare and a firm believer in the restorative properties of scent, once wrote. And it is said that Charles VI of France used to sit on cushions stuffed with the perfumed leaves and flowers of lavender when he wanted to clear his brain.

With the new interest in natural health remedies on the rise, the ancient art of aromatherapy is being rediscovered and revived. Aromatherapists claim that when inhaled, the chemical constituents of fragrance molecules found in a plant's essential oils stimulate the olfactory nerve centers in the nose and find their way immediately, through the body's biochemical pathways, to the part of the brain that regulates emotions, as well as to other body organs. Forest air, for

A branch of herbal medicine, aromatherapy is believed to have originated in ancient China or perhaps in Vedic India. Terracotta flasks containing traces of fragrance oils from plants have been dated back about five thousand years to the Egyptians, who are known to have used the fragrant extracts of marjoram,

instance, which is now sold canned in Japan, has been found to contain substances that, inhaled, enhance concentration and combat fatigue. These are the same substances used by the trees in their defense against microorganisms and insects. So, when we bring scents in from the world outdoors, we are literally borrowing nature's own survival mechanisms to help us survive our fast-paced, stress-inducing world.

In some homes the tradition of drying herbs continues. Bunches of leaves and flowers can be found filling baskets or hanging decoratively from ceiling beams, antique drying racks, blanket stands, even from ladders suspended horizontally from a ceiling. Bunches of herbs can be hung from a sinuous branch placed across the fireplace—a sweet-smelling display in the summertime, while in the winter the heat of the fire encourages the release of the herbal fragrance. Whether or not these scents have any curative value, they are a natural antidote to the spiritless home.

Although many flowers and leaves are fragrant, the oils found in the petals, leaves, bark, or roots of various plants contain highly concentrated doses of beneficial smells—it takes a ton (1000 kilos) of rose petals to produce 520 grams of essence. Today, these oils are sometimes used to scent decorative candles and to heighten the aroma of potpourris or dried flower arrangements. The essential oils of certain roses, besides making the room smell pleasant, are said to relieve stress and depression. Sweet-smelling oil of jasmine, whose petals are harvested at midnight when the flower is most highly scented, was used extensively in ancient Eastern cultures as an antidepressive; the Chinese used to put branches of jasmine in bedrooms at night because they believed that it could counteract an oppressive mood. Closer to our own outdoors, the fresh scent of lavender oil is believed to relax the body and promote sleep.

Perhaps, as new concerns about toxicity persuade us to turn increasingly to decorating products based on natural substances (sales of natural paints and varnishes, for instance, are rising rapidly) houses will smell better, and the scents of nature brought indoors will have less of a battle for our attention. Plants are apparently effective in absorbing a variety of airborne pollutants.

Creeping greenery helps freshen the air in a tiny home office, above, which occupies the corner of an urban conservatory.

The Perfumed Home

THE SCENT OF THE OUTDOORS

The more the outside is brought indoors for the purposes of furnishing, finishing, and decorating the home, the more the sense of smell can allow itself to profit from those leaf and flower fragrances that nature offers, and which lovers of scent like Ruth Beebe Wilder have celebrated as being "an added joy in happy times and gently remedial when life seems warped and tired." Some people add cedar chips, sandalwood, pinecones, or even lavender to the wood burned in the fireplace in order to sweeten the smell of fire and room. Others are now replacing the use of chemically based polishes with beeswax, which is often scented with lemon balm, myrtle, or sweet marjoram; sweet cecily seeds were once used by the English to make an oil for polishing oak floors, giving them a good shine and a pleasant scent.

Some natural floor coverings and other treatments, too, can emit scents to add to the enjoyment of plants or flowers brought indoors. The roots of cus-cus, from India, are woven into sun shades and sprinkled with water on hot days to give off a cooling, myrrh-like scent.

In fact, many kinds of grasses, though generally known for

Bundles of lavender are placed in the fireplace in an English farmhouse, opposite. In winter, they are burned to fill the room with a sweet, tantalizing scent. Flowers are easily air-dried when inverted and hung from the ceiling, above. A living, fragrant valance, below, is a delightful summertime sculpture in a suburban home.

their texture rather than their scent, are very sweet smelling. Sweet grass, used by Native Americans to make baskets and mats, gives a strong, sweet and very long-lasting aroma reminiscent of fresh hay. Traditionally, it was used as a perfume and burned as incense in connection with the ritual sun dance. In Europe, it was strewn on festival days—which is why it is also known as holy grass. In Iceland, sweet grass was tied in bundles and hung in rooms for its scent, while in Sweden the bundles would be tied over the bed to ensure good sleep.

Lemongrass, grown in pots, adds a citrus touch to a kitchen. Sweet annie is one of the most fragrant herbs available; it is a shrub that can grow quite high, and the imaginative proprietors of one Pennsylvania herb farm use it as a holiday tree, instead of evergreen each year. Even willow branches, brought indoors and bundled decoratively, give a refreshing scent reminiscent of the rivers beside which these trees grow.

Fragrant, dried flower arrangements, sometimes combining a variety of scented flowers, leaves, and grasses, can be particularly evocative. Oliver Wendell Holmes, former chief justice of

An antique French "tree of life" candelabra with leaves, branches, and
scented candles, previous page, left, is a unique and magnificent design element
in a dining room. When its fragrant candles are lit, they complement the lemony
smell of nearby geraniums. A harvest of dried flowers fills the air with scent in
a gardener's studio in the English countryside, previous page, right.

Fragrant French lavender grows indoors at a dried flower shop in
Warwickshire, England, above left. The aromatic wall arrangement features
purple marjoram, goldenrod, onion heads, rambling rose, reindeer
moss, and a garden rake on a bed of sweet-smelling hay. A simple
dresser, above right, is festooned with dried flowers and culinary herbs.

the United States Supreme Court, once wrote of everlastings: "Perhaps the herb everlasting, the fragrant imortelle of our autumn fields, has the most suggestive odour to me of all that set me dreaming. I can hardly describe the strange thoughts and emotions that come to me as I inhale the aroma of its pale, dry, rustling flowers."

Potpourris, with their sensual, Provençal heritage, are another way that the scent of the outdoors has traditionally been introduced into the home. Some combination of herbs, flowers, leaves, berries, wood chips, spices, citrus peels, and essential oils is combined with a fixative to create a feast of color and fragrance. One time-tested recipe from Provence calls for various kinds of roses, acacia, heads of pinks, violets, lily of the valley, blue and white lilac, orange and lemon blossoms, mignonette, heliotrope, narcissi, jonquil, and small quantities of balm, rosemary, thyme, and myrtle. But a variety of blends have been developed in recent years, focus-

Mixing bowls filled with personal blends of potpourri, right, bring the scents of the country into an urban townhouse.

Vines, gathered in the nearby New England woods, were woven together
with highly scented dried peonies into a naturally fragrant canopy for this
Victorian-style four-poster bed, above and below. Ferns help freshen
the air and control humidity.

ing, for example, on the stimulating scents of lemon, orange, or tangerine, or the nostalgic scents of violet, sweet pea and heather.

A potpourri mix can be like a microcosm in scent of a specific natural environment: an herb-garden potpourri, for instance, composed of kitchen herbs; or a woodland mix combining the aromas of sassafras, pine, balsam, and berries. Potpourri can evoke the seasons too: the lighter scents of daffodil, hyacinth, peach, and magnolia for the early days of spring; the more heady, sultry aromas of jasmine, rose, and chrysanthemum for the summer; for the fall, myrtle, sandalwood, and bayberry.

One of the exciting things about scent in nature is its variability. By contrast, there is something static and "dead" about the artificial scents that modern chemistry has been producing since the end of the nineteenth century. The fragrances of the natural world work in unison both with temperature and humidity, and with the sun and moon: most people can smell the weather with their eyes closed if they are in a natural environment. Some dried flowers, such as roses, become especially fragrant in a warm room, since warmth encourages the release of essential oils into the atmosphere. Bring twigs of flowering sugar maple into the warmth and they emit a spring-like fragrance. Moisture, too, will effect the yielding of scent: fragrance increases before a storm. Cedar becomes especially aromatic in a steamy atmosphere (the steam from a shower releases its fragrance).

We tend to associate flower scents with daylight, when petals open to the sun. But some— such as nicotiana, or tobacco plant, night-scented stock, and jasmine—known in India as moonlight of the grove— respond to the moon. The night-scented tube rose, whose white flowers glow luminous in darkness, was once valued for indoor cultivation until it became popular as a funeral flower. These plants, grown indoors, fill the evening hours with a sweetness that few day-scented flowers can match: Lotus, a water plant, is said to have its roots in the mud, while its fragrance reaches the throne of God. The bright, rose-colored flowers of sand verbena, used in hanging baskets, yield a strong honey-like scent toward evening. They scent the house into the night, perhaps inducing pleasant dreams of nature.

In this modern New York apartment, below, dried grasses and fixtures constructed with whitewashed timber from a dismantled barn help to impart the scent of nature to city life.

Chapter Four

THE SOUND
OF THE
OUTDOORS

No wind, yet the musical low murmur through the pines,
quite pronounced, curious, like waterfalls.

—WALT WHITMAN, *SPECIMEN DAYS*

THERE IS AN OMINOUSLY SI-lent area of bone-dry dunes in California's Death Valley, where lives a species of bird whose song precisely mimics the sound of running water. To hear that song move over the parched sand is to be seized by a mixture of intense sensations. Closing your eyes to listen, the sound transports you, in your imagination, far from this California desert depression, to the edge of a sparkling mountain stream where you can almost feel the water run through your fingers, see it glisten in the sun, taste it as it wets the dryness in your throat.

Just as the bird's song helps to create in the desert an imaginary oasis where the needs of the spirit, if not the body, can be met, so sounds of nature brought into the home can open the indoor environment to the world of the wild. These are sounds of living things in motion, and people have been introducing them into outdoor gardens and courtyards for thousands of years, not only by building fountains, but also by growing certain trees and grasses whose leaves whisper in the breeze, and by attracting birds for their song. Now, at a time when living takes place predominately indoors, and when ev-ery attention is being given to combating feelings of sterility in the home by creating more natural living environments, the option of bringing the sounds of nature inside is one being increasingly explored.

Hearing is a sense subtly and intricately connected with other sensory experiences, giving sound the power to move us in the richest way possible. We are "touched" by what we hear in the most literal, if imperceptible, way; the skin actually responds to the pressure of sound waves, and "deep touch" receptors around muscles and ligaments in the human body are also receptive to resonance.

Most powerfully, the sense of hearing is linked through our imaginations with the sense of sight, to the extent that visual and auditory experiences not only reinforce each other, but can virtually substitute for one another. The German expressionist architect Eric Mendelsohn used to design buildings while listening to Bach, allowing the music to inspire him in his visualizations. Certainly, many visual artists and some writers find their creative powers heightened when certain types of music are played.

Water in a fast-moving creek, previous page, produces a rhythmic sound that invites quiet, contemplative thought. A copper wind chime with a weathered patina makes music as wind wafts in through open windows, above. Sounds of the garden become part of the indoor experience, opposite.

Nature's Music

This recirculating water fountain was ordered in kit form, above. Although the fountain is small, the gentle sound of water falling on seashells and river pebbles fills the room.

Nature's own music, with its random rhythms and melodies, has the same power to construct visual meaning in the mind of the hearer, and to call up intense, though often subconscious, emotional responses.

Sounds of wind and water move through the air, filling it. They are not limited by any precise location. Like music, which the mind hears best when the eyes are closed, such natural sounds isolated from visual experience can suggest to the imagination visual scenes of great lyrical or dramatic quality: scenes whose scope may seem vaster than any vistas seen by the eye—images of immense, limitless oceans of space. The sound of the wind as it whips through the trees and across fields evokes spaces so wide and open that they seem to have no boundaries at all.

These sounds and images of infinity, experienced most clearly during those still moments when the body comes to rest, are especially conducive to quiet reflection. They are typically low-frequency sounds, the type that the human brain finds most relaxing. It is interesting that in the austere abbeys of the Middle Ages, it was in the "paradises" reserved for monks' religious contemplation that water fountains were installed, since their gentle, flowing sounds were believed to inspire thoughts of a universal nature.

Only recently has a scientific understanding developed of how sound, like daylight, contributes both to psychological and physical well-being. Studies of the way in which various frequencies, rhythms, and amplitudes affect the human mind and body have shown that even on a purely physiological level, the sounds of nature tend to be the most restful and fulfilling, while the most distressing and ultimately damaging are invariably created by machine. With this understanding has come a new emphasis on natural sound in the indoor environment, and a critical listening to the spaces in which we live.

Whether we realize it or not, we do hear all the time, even in sleep. In fact, the ear is so sensitive that it can almost hear the random sound of air molecules vibrating against the eardrum. Given this sensitivity, it's not surprising that the mind can so easily become exhausted from the constant stimulation of traffic humming outside, or from noise invading from a neighboring apartment, that it soon learns to filter out the sound, along with other sensory experiences. In other words, in a noisy, urban environment we tend to deaden our receptivity to sound. On the other hand, a room sealed off from the outside world by double glazing will have as a background sound a dead, oppressive silence—the kind that in nature only exists during the calm before a storm. It is a silence that creates feelings of restlessness and isolation, with every little noise only emphasizing these feelings.

We have many options at our disposal to create a sense of life in our homes. Whether doors and windows are flung open to the sounds of the garden, a water sculpture is installed in the living room, wind chimes are hung to catch each passing breeze, or audio recordings are played of soft rain falling in the tropical forest, these things are done with the understanding that sounds that reproduce the auditory experience provided by nature help us to feel at home in our homes.

The random rhythm of a fire is one of nature's most comforting sounds. Building a crackling fire can be a pleasurable, almost ceremonial act. A traditional hearth surrounded by specialized tools reflects the intricacies of fire building, above. Sculpted by nature, seashells evoke the sounds of the ocean, left.

Wind Play

Many of the methods for bringing nature's sounds indoors were first explored in gardens. Wooden whirligigs, once popular as audio defense systems in the war between gardeners and birds, are finding a new popularity as instruments played by indoor, rather than outdoor, breezes. They can be found sticking up from planters, their bright colors spinning as they hum. Wind chimes made from metal, clay, bamboo, glass, or shells—each material producing its own distinctive sound—have long hung in gardens and on porches, the chimes moved to music by passing breezes. Their pure tones are powerfully evocative of the moods inspired by particular landscapes—high and whimsical like water dancing over river pebbles, or deep, mysterious, and vast.

Legend has it that wind chimes were developed in China, after a certain medicine man, tired of shaking the gourd whose sound was believed to cure the sick, fashioned the first chime from an inverted water jug. Whatever the truth of this legend, we do know that tuned wind chimes existed in China four thousand years ago, when ornamental stones were selected not only for their visual qualities, but also for the sound they made when struck. Among the most sought after were certain flat, plain stones known as "floating chimes from the banks of the Si River," which were hung in special sacred places for their pure musical tones. In many parts of the Far East, chimes were believed to have magically protective qualities capable of driving away evil spirits; some believed their music to be the whisperings of Buddha.

Positioned near a breezeway, whirligigs are entertaining objects, opposite above. Wind chimes are hung from a branch brought indoors, opposite below. A South American wind machine catches the breeze in this city loft, right.

Today, new designs in wind chimes may focus on particular themes. A series of "harbor bells," made from angular pieces of steel, reproduces the haunting notes of various buoys that float in New England harbors. Others, such as the chimes created by musician John Stannard, are tuned according to the structure of Eastern scales, calling to mind the exotic heritage of these primitive wind instruments, and the distant lands where they first played for human ears.

Water Play

Wind chimes speak of nature, providing musical evidence of an elemental energy that permeates the outdoor world. The sound of water is the sound of nature itself, and its changing patterns, so familiar to human experience, are universally fascinating. Water is a life force running through the human body and covering two-thirds of the earth's surface, as crucial to survival as the air we breathe. No wonder, then, that human civilization has since its earliest days gone to great lengths to introduce both the sound and sight of water into daily life.

In the East water sources were once held sacred: the Byzantine water works represented the tree of life itself. But fountains served many purposes. In the Middle East, where the sound of water first entered the ordered domain of gardens, and in ancient Rome and Greece, water fountains carved out of stone served as architectural ornament, while cooling and humidifying the air during the fierce heat of the day. In southern Spain, the Moors created stunning effects with water at the Alhambra Palace, where shallow ribbons of water traversed the tiled courtyards, shimmering like silk in the sunlight. And in the hallway of the adobe Pyramid House, a contemporary home in sun-parched Arizona, a narrow canal of water cuts a path down the center of a long, stepped hallway tiled in stone, moving slowly on the landings and cascading gently as it reaches the shallow steps.

In the towns of Pompeii and Herculaneum, water was brought indoors. Relics of stone water fountains and simple, rectangular pools in the atria of many houses have been excavated from the ruins. They testify to the powerful contrast achieved by combining water and stone, the one dense and motionless, the other diffuse and fluid. Later, in the sixteenth century, diners at the Villa Lante sat around a massive stone banqueting table and may have floated their dishes along a channel of water that ran down its center.

Though most of us cannot endeavor to re-create the splendor of the classical past, we can at least introduce certain elements in our homes that evoke a timeless, sensory feeling. Today mail-order fountain kits are available from garden suppliers, complete with recirculating pumps and PVC liners. With these, any receptacle capable of holding weight is a potential self-contained, babbling foun-

In this small Manhattan sun room the architect designed a recirculating water fountain set into the wall to conserve precious space, opposite.

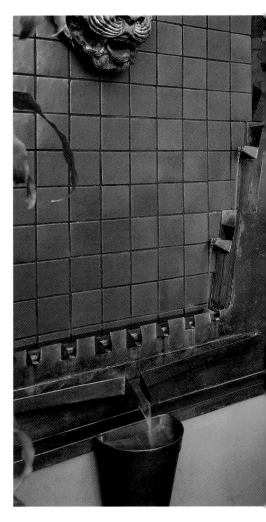

The cleverly designed fountain, above, produces a variety of sounds as the water cascades down both sides and trickles from the spout into the basin below.

tain, with rocks or river pebbles and even water plants hiding the electrical works. Such devices can help connect our homes with the glory of the past.

The introduction of recirculating pumps has also revived the art of water sculpture, although now concrete or fiberglass may replace stone and terra-cotta, and many include electronic controls that can be programmed to determine and change the flow sequence and the sound. Antique and reproduction spouts are available, and many of the new water sculptures are more abstract in design, in keeping with the pure quality of water. Instead of lion's heads and grotesque masks, or the cupids of Victorian times, today's water sculptures may represent elemental forms.

A geometrical recycling water sculpture, right, stands in an urban hallway. Water gushes across river pebbles, from one level to the next, producing an effect not unlike that of a mountain brook. Residents of a Manhattan apartment can relax in the tub while enjoying the gently therapeutic sound of water flowing across a sheet of corrugated metal set into the wall, opposite. The rate of flow can be regulated for a softer or louder sound.

There are many forms of water play, and each produces a different quality of sound. Running water produces what is known as "white noise"—a sound that contains all the frequencies in the audible spectrum, just as white light contains all the wavelengths in the visible spectrum. This makes it an ideal background sound, perfect for masking those invasive sounds of the city, and equally effective in making a silent, sound-proofed home feel less isolated. There is the babbling of a fountain, the gush of water flowing from a gargoyle, or the lazy splash of a dripping well—a circular pool half vaulted over into which water spouts.

The size of the nozzle itself influences the sound of a fountain or spout, with narrow nozzles producing a delicate tinklé, and wide nozzles an almost thunderous gush. Materials are important too. For example, a sculpture set into the wall of an urban bathroom uses water flowing down a sheet of corrugated tin for a gentle, murmuring effect.

In some water sculptures, the interference of carefully placed rocks causes gurgles in the pattern of sound, like the gurgling of a creek. We can learn much from waterfalls, whose tones vary according to certain placements of rocks and other natural disturbances, as well as the lie of the land. Other substances can be manipulated to create the sound of water: The architect Charles Moore claims to be able to create the sound of a babbling brook by tuning a serrated copper "weir" with pliers.

Unlike those forms of water play that produce white noise, the Japanese "ping" fountain produces a pure sound composed of a succession of single notes. Drops of water fall, one by one, from a spout into a stone projecting from the wall beneath. Since the stone has only the slightest dip in its surface, water overflows from it, drop by drop, into a lower basin, and then into a lower one again, each drop producing a different tone.

In Japan, the simple, restrained melody produced by the ping fountain is believed to create an atmosphere of pure peace and tranquility, just as the fountains in medieval monastic gardens inspired the monks.

It was not only the fountains, but also the stone abbeys themselves that provided a special kind of auditory experience— the experience of sound reverberating richly off the hard, articulated surfaces of walls, floors, and ceilings. Many ancient churches, with their fantastically ribbed ceilings, their almost shell-like alcoves, and their massive stone construction, are acoustical instruments in their own right, and the quality of sound they produce is similar to a canyon's haunting echoes.

The materials typically used nowadays in the construction and furnishing of homes—the plastics and synthetics—produce a deadened, homogenous sound without character.

Surfaces respond to sound waves, with natural materials creating the most distinctive acoustical effects. Like a cave, a stone-floored room without draperies will have a hard, reverberating sound—a deeply resonant but somewhat cold effect, not unlike singing in a tiled bathroom. On the other hand, a woody room with carpet, cork flooring or matting (leafy or not), and natural fabric or other fiber on the walls will absorb and hold sound, softening it.

Probably the simplest, most poetic expression of the acoustical properties of natural forms and materials is the cowrie shell. Brought indoors from the beach and displayed for its glossy, decorated surface, it comes to life when, lifted to the ear, sound reverberates in its hard, rounded interior. Suddenly the ocean is everywhere. The waves crash, foaming surf whispers, and the wind wails. This is the sound of nature: a perfect illusion of the ever-changing patterns we hear in the wild.

This living room in a small Philadelphia home, opposite, is far from the ocean. But, held to the ear, some of the shells collected in the wicker basket might provide an illusion of waves lapping against the shoreline. Cork, made from the outer bark of the cork oak, lines the window ledge, softening and helping to absorb the sounds of the city outside.

In this New Hampshire kitchen, above, a fieldstone floor and counter not only help to intensify the sound of water as it splashes into the sink, but also are visually evocative of the natural world, where water and stone are so often paired.

Chapter Five

THE TASTE OF THE OUTDOORS

The scene is bathed in moonlight,
the wind whispers.
The moonlight plays quietly
over lute and books,
the wind ruffles a half-circle
of Autumn water.
We feel a pure atmosphere
around our table and seats;
the common dust of the world
is far from our souls.

—JI CHENG,
THE CRAFT OF GARDEN

IT IS VIRTUALLY IMPOSSIBLE TO duplicate precisely the experience of eating out of doors. The moon or the sun, the balmy air and dappled light; the sounds of bird song in spring and summer or of autumn's crackling fire; the smoky scents of mesquite and hickory—nothing can quite compare with these environmental "dining rooms." Though inimitable, it may be possible to capture the essence of the experience, and in this way bring the outdoors in at mealtime.

There is something inherently casual about outdoor dining, a casualness that inspires warm conviviality. Any attempts at formality are subverted by the unpredictable events of nature. The table might be set with the best china and silverware, awaiting guests, when a sudden flurry of wind dumps a trail of leaves over the careful arrangement. A cheeseboard or plate of hors d'oeuvres might be decorated randomly with autumnal foliage or wildflowers to suit the season. Whatever the setting, elements of the surrounding landscape are interwoven in the outdoor table, and the same effects can be mimicked indoors. Natural table decorations include an assemblage of gilt and natural pomegranates and pine cones during the holidays; a twig-and-moss centerpiece embedded with a votive candle holder; and a table "cloth" of preserved or freshly fallen autumn leaves covered with glass, to name just a few possibilities.

One of the joys of eating in the open air is to be surrounded by nature's sheer abundance. Be it the controlled profusion of the garden or the unchecked vitality of the wild, it can hardly fail to stimulate the appetite. At the 1991 Art Expo in New York City, "Art: Designs for Living," a Manhattan floral design firm called VSF created an idealized "Garden of Earthly Delights"—a setting so luxuriant it seemed designed to tempt the viewer into tasting apples in the scene! A path, defined by a border of pansies, meandered to a dining table ringed with seats made of tree trunks and overhung by a tree whose branches held light bulbs under beige silk shades. The "dishes" on the table were large leaves and blossoms. If any reference was intended here to the fantastically dark vision described by Bosch in his painting of the same name, it was to the unfettered sensual enjoyment that we find in nature.

In a Mediterranean kitchen, culinary implements made from clearly natural materials are displayed against a tile backdrop painted in earthy tones, previous page. Rose hips, above, can be made into tea or jam, or even used for delightful topiaries in diminutive pots. Dining on an enclosed sunporch surrounded by plants gives the illusion of relaxing alfresco, opposite.

Human beings thrived for thousands of years on a diet gathered in the wild, on local leaves, roots, shoots, nuts and berries, fruits and blossoms. In fact, there are over eighty thousand kinds of edible plants in existence today (although as wild land is cleared, these plants are rapidly disappearing from the world), and any picnic is almost certain to be surrounded by the makings of a plentiful meal and by a multitude of different and surprising tastes.

Brought inside, these tastes form the basis of a new "wild cuisine." Previously unknown mushrooms and leafy herbs—like wild ginger and the spinach-like herb lamb's quarters—are becoming widely available, gathered with a salvaged knowledge of foraging that was practically second sense to our ancestors—a very detailed understanding of what kinds of environments certain varieties prefer, and how to identify them. Although a few of these wild foods are now being cultivated, most are untamable, insisting on growing wherever they want, as long as no human influence is involved. Mushrooms in particular, coveted since ancient times (the Romans called them "the food of the gods"), have eluded culti-

Creating artful arrangements of fruit and flowers brings a sense of nature's abundance indoors, above. Herbs also provide endless decorating options, whether woven into garlands or crafted into edible wreaths for kitchen use.

vation. Seaweeds are also being appreciated for their complex, salty tastes and rich nutritious content.

Pure and uncompromising in their tastes and textures, these foods are being used by innovative cooks to create simple, casual dishes that satisfy both the palate and the eye, while clearly evoking the outdoors. Wild food is indigenous food, an integral part of the immediate environment; the fiddlehead fern served at the table may be the offspring of plants that have grown for thousands of years in the woods in which you walk, where the tree that is your tabletop might have been felled.

To list the names of just some of the flowers that have been served in various societies conjures up images of hedgerows and fields, bowers and garden beds. Hibiscus, jasmine, lotus, and orange blossom flowers have been made into teas by the Chinese for centuries, and chrysanthemums into soups and salads. The Romans scented their red wine with dark red roses, and used lavender and calendula in food. The Elizabethans served up fragrant pinks and honeysuckle, hay-like clover, primroses, honey-flavored cowslips, and scented violets.

Now that the taste for flowers is in a period of revival, they are being grown organically especially for culinary purposes, both commercially and in private garden beds, pots, and window boxes. Some growers are now cultivating edible flowers year-round in the greenhouse, often through hydroponic means.

For those who want to bring the barbecue indoors, an indoor fireplace can provide some of the elements of the traditional outdoor feast. Colonial Americans used the fireplace for their day-to-day stewing, baking, and slow roasting, either placing the food directly on a grate over the flames or stewing it in a large, suspended pot. A peeled branch of green maple or hickory, turned by hand, was used to roast meats over the fire. With its sweet smells, its gentle crackling sound, and its mesmerizing flicker, the cooking fire provided warmth, conversation, and a delicious dinner all in one.

The collection of recipes that follow were gathered from health-conscious chefs and food professionals who believe that a dish can look as exquisite as it tastes, and provide nutrients as well. All of the recipes emphasize the bounty and variety of the outdoors.

MESCLUN WITH HAZELNUT VINAIGRETTE

Serves 6

Lettuces have been with us since earliest times as the basis for salads. One famous epicurean of ancient Rome is said to have sprinkled the lettuces growing in his garden with wine and honey to make them even more flavorful! Epicureans today are more likely to fill the salad bowl with *mesclun* for a flavorful and colorful side dish.

Mesclun is a blend of many varieties of baby lettuce and field greens, aromatic herbs, and edible flowers created first in the French countryside. Although

many of the ingredients can be found in the wild or the garden, most people buy freshly mixed *mesclun* from greenmarkets or specialty fresh produce stores. The combination of sharp and sweet flavors and bright floral and rich green colors creates a salad that is as attractive and healthful as it is appetizing.

½ POUND *MESCLUN* (BABY LETTUCES, ARUGULA, BASIL, NASTURTIUM FLOWERS AND LEAVES, ROSE PETALS, CALENDULA BLOSSOMS, LAMB'S-QUARTERS)

HAZELNUT VINAIGRETTE

¼ CUP HAZELNUT OIL

2 TABLESPOONS RICE OR WINE VINEGAR

SALT AND FRESHLY GROUND BLACK PEPPER TO TASTE

Whisk vinaigrette ingredients together. Toss with salad just before serving.

Fresh flowers are more than beautiful—many are useful in the kitchen. The sunflower, above, yields oil and nutritious seeds. The seeds are wonderful alone, but especially good with salads and healthful fruit shakes.

SAUTÉED WILD MUSHROOMS

〜〜〜

Serves 4

A partial tree stump acts as a bracket in the corner of a country pantry, above. Some natural-object aficionados especially seek out mushroom- and moss-covered logs and branches for interior display.

Antonio Carluccio, whose Neal Street Restaurant in London's Soho specializes in dishes featuring natural foods, is an avid mycophile, or "mushroom lover." He can confidently identify the many species of edible fungi that hide among pine needles on forest floors, nestle in the nooks and crannies of tree trunks, or grow scattered in moist meadows. Much of his free time is spent on mushroom-foraging expeditions, from which he returns with baskets full of fungi for the pantry.

This dish of mixed sautéed mushrooms can be served as an appetizer, as a complement to a light, roasted or grilled fish or meat dish, or with scrambled eggs for a simple lunch or supper. It features five species of mushroom: rubber brush mushrooms (*Hydnum repandum*), which thrive under pine trees; chanterelles (*Cantharellus cibarius*), found on mossy ground; gray or oyster mushroom (*Pleurotus ostreatus*), which grows on tree trunks; parasole mushrooms (*Lepiota procera*), found under pine trees and in fields; and black, fluted horns of plenty (*Craterellus cornucopioides*), gathered from bare soil, whose flavor is enhanced by drying and then reconstituting the mushrooms. If you are not knowledgeable about mushrooms, it would be virtually impossible to identify the many species found in the wild. But an increasing number of mushrooms are available in specialty food stores or even for growing in your home garden.

To prepare mushrooms for eating, give them a quick water rinse; alternatively, wipe with a damp towel. Cut off any blemishes. In general, remove stems of chanterelles, gray mushrooms, and parasol mushrooms.

1 POUND MIXED WILD MUSHROOMS, CLEANED AND DESTEMMED, WHERE APPROPRIATE

1 CLOVE GARLIC, FINELY CHOPPED

4 TABLESPOONS OLIVE OIL

1 TABLESPOON FINELY CHOPPED PARSLEY

SALT TO TASTE

Sauté the mushrooms and garlic in very hot oil or a combination of oil and butter, stirring constantly, for about 3 minutes, until you see that the mushrooms are just cooked. They should still be firm and slightly crackly. Do not overcook, or the mushrooms will lose water. For best results, stir-fry in a Chinese wok. Upon serving, add parsley and salt.

EGGPLANT AND BELL PEPPER TERRINE

❧

Serves 6

The perfect beauty of nature's lines makes a versatile, if ephemeral, design element, opposite.

This appetizer is the first dish of a three-part feast combining wild and garden-grown produce. Devised by Dan Lenchner and Joni Greenspan of Manna Catering, New York, this terrine and their other two courses for dinner party fare celebrate the outdoor world in the most elegant way. *Mesclun* salad (page 108) would also be a perfect complement to the meal.

Dan suggests serving the terrine with very crusty bread and garnishing it with finely diced peppers. An additional garnish of flowering rosemary accents the Mediterranean flavor of the ingredients.

3 MEDIUM EGGPLANTS

3 RED BELL PEPPERS

3 YELLOW BELL PEPPERS

3 GOLDEN (ORANGE) BELL PEPPERS

3 GREEN BELL PEPPERS

HERBED OIL (ROSEMARY-INFUSED OLIVE OIL IS USED HERE)

SALT AND FRESHLY GROUND BLACK PEPPER TO TASTE

Line a medium loaf pan (approximately 9 × 3 × 3 inches) with plastic wrap. Set aside. Preheat the broiler.

Slice the unpeeled eggplants in half-inch pieces, salt the slices, and let them stand in a colander for about an hour. (Salt encourages the bitter juices to drain off.)

Seed the peppers and slice them into thirds. Brush the slices with half of the herbed oil. Broil the sliced and oiled peppers until the skins are just black; turn and repeat. Remove from broiler and place in paper bags, separating each color into its own bag. Allow the peppers to cool.

Meanwhile, rinse and pat dry the eggplant slices and brush them with the remaining oil. Broil and set aside.

When the peppers are cool, remove the skins. Slice the eggplant and peppers into pieces that will fit your loaf pan. Arrange two layers of each vegetable in the pan and sprinkle salt between each layer.

Wrap the filled pan well, weigh down lightly, and refrigerate the terrine overnight. When you are ready to serve it, slice it with a sharp, thin-bladed knife, electric if possible.

Leftover masonry from a dismantled patio was cleverly recycled as a rustic wine rack, opposite.

WARM BEET, GOAT CHEESE, AND POTATO GALETTES

ᴄᴏᴏᴏᴏ

Serves 4

This recipe was devised by Chef Alan Harding at Nosmo King, a New York restaurant specializing in regional and organic foods based on locally produced ingredients from nearby greenmarkets. Here he takes beets and goat cheese and gives them a new interpretation with a sprightly vinaigrette.

1 LARGE BAKING POTATO, PEELED AND CUT INTO ⅛-INCH SLICES

2 MEDIUM-SIZED BEETS, ROASTED IN A 350° OVEN FOR 2 TO 2½ HOURS

SALT AND FRESHLY GROUND BLACK PEPPER TO TASTE

8 OUNCES SPREADABLE GOAT CHEESE

ARUGULA LEAVES FOR GARNISH

CITRUS VINAIGRETTE (RECIPE FOLLOWS)

Boil the potato slices in salted water until tender. Remove from heat and plunge into cold water.

Drain and reserve.

Peel the roasted beets and cut into ⅛-inch slices. Reserve.

On a cookie sheet place four 4-inch ring molds (size is approximate—biscuit cutters can be used instead). The molds will temporarily hold the tart shape. In each mold, place four slices of potato. Season with salt and pepper. Over the potato slices on each tart spread ¼ of the goat cheese, and top it with 6 beet slices. Warm the molds in a 350° oven for 3 minutes.

Remove from oven. With a spatula, lift each tart in its ring mold from the cookie sheet and place on a dish. Remove mold. Garnish with arugula leaves, and dribble with citrus vinaigrette. The petal-like garnish in the picture is a beet purée.

CITRUS VINAIGRETTE

1 OUNCE ORANGE JUICE

1 OUNCE LEMON JUICE

1 OUNCE LIME JUICE

2 OUNCES OLIVE OIL

1 TEASPOON CORIANDER SEEDS

½ ORANGE, SECTIONED

SALT AND FRESHLY GROUND WHITE PEPPER TO TASTE

Blend the ingredients together and season with salt and pepper.

COHO SALMON WITH WILD RICE AND WILD MUSHROOMS

Serves 6

For a main course, Manna Catering answers the call of the wild with a dish whose ingredients come from river, woodland, and marsh. It is there that the wild rice grows not as a rice at all, but as a grass seed. Native Americans of Minnesota and Wisconsin once harvested the wild seeds, navigating the marshes by canoe. Only in the past few years has this food yielded to attempts to cultivate it.

6 WHOLE COHO SALMON, 10–12 OUNCES EACH, FILLETED

COURT BOUILLON (RECIPE FOLLOWS)

1 CUP WILD RICE

1 BUNCH SCALLIONS, GREEN PART ONLY

¼ CUP OLIVE OIL

½ CUP PINE NUTS, ROASTED

1 POUND MIXED WILD MUSHROOMS, CLEANED AND DESTEMMED, WHERE APPROPRIATE

¼ CUP BUTTER

SALT AND COARSELY GROUND BLACK PEPPER TO TASTE

Poach the salmon in *court bouillon*: bring liquid to a simmer, immerse the fish, and simmer 10 minutes per inch of thickness. Let cool to room temperature and skin. Set aside and cover with plastic wrap.

Boil the rice in a quart of salted water until the kernels just begin to split, about 40 minutes. Drain and rinse with cold water.

While the rice cooks, slice the scallions, reserving twelve, into 4-inch pieces. Sauté the scallions in the olive oil until they turn bright green, then add the pine nuts and rice, and cook, stirring, for a moment.

Sauté the mushrooms in the butter until softened. Add salt and pepper.

To dress each plate: Lay salmon horizontally in the middle of the plate. Wrap two of the reserved scallion pieces around each fish. Spoon rice onto the top of the plate and mushrooms along the bottom.

Artifacts of the countryside—milk pitchers and cheese wheels— become collector's items when brought indoors and displayed.

COURT BOUILLON

1 QUART WATER

1 CARROT

1 OR MORE ONIONS

SALT AND FRESHLY GROUND BLACK PEPPER TO TASTE

Bring mixture of all ingredients to a boil and simmer for 20 to 30 minutes. Strain.

NAPOLEONS OF AUTUMN VEGETABLES WITH CARROT SAUCE

Serves 4

This layered vegetable dish from Chef Harding, with its distinctly autumnal color, serves as a reminder of the changing seasons. During the summer months, substitute spinach and grilled zucchini for the greens in this recipe.

FILLING

4 LARGE PORTOBELLO
MUSHROOMS

SALT AND FRESHLY
GROUND BLACK PEPPER
TO TASTE

OLIVE OIL

1 CLOVE GARLIC,
CRUSHED

1 POUND ASSORTED
WINTER GREENS,
SUCH AS COLLARD
GREENS, CHICORY, OR
ESCAROLE, RINSED,
DRIED, AND TORN INTO
PIECES

3 SHEETS FILO
(AVAILABLE IN FROZEN
FOOD SECTION OF
MARKET)

DUXELLES

2 POUNDS WHITE
MUSHROOMS, WIPED
CLEAN AND THINLY
SLICED

1 TEASPOON EXTRA-
VIRGIN OLIVE OIL

CARROT SAUCE

2 CUPS CARROT JUICE

2 TABLESPOONS EXTRA-
VIRGIN OLIVE OIL

SALT AND FRESHLY
GROUND BLACK PEPPER
TO TASTE

CHERVIL SPRIGS FOR
GARNISH

Filling: Preheat oven to 350°F. Season the portobello mushrooms with salt and pepper, coat them lightly with olive oil, and grill, or braise them in the oven until tender.

In a large skillet heat 1 tablespoon olive oil until hot and add the garlic. Cook, stirring, until lightly browned and remove. Add the greens and sauté them until slightly wilted. Season with salt and pepper and remove skillet from heat.

Using 1 thawed filo sheet at a time, brush one side of it with olive oil and season it with salt and pepper. Place the filo on a cookie sheet and prepare the remaining sheets in the same manner, stacking them on top of the first. Weight the stack by placing another cookie sheet over it. Bake for 6 minutes, or until the pastry is lightly browned. Remove filo sheets from the oven and cut into 3-inch squares with a serrated knife.

Duxelles: In a large skillet heat the extra-virgin olive oil until hot, add the white mushrooms, and cook them, tossing, until just softened. Season with salt and pepper. Transfer to a food processor and chop finely, but not into a purée.

Carrot sauce: In a large saucepan bring the carrot juice to a boil. Stir in the extra-virgin olive oil, and salt and pepper to taste. Blend at high speed in a blender until fully combined.

To assemble the napoleons: On each serving plate, place 1 tablespoon of the mushroom *duxelles*. Top with a filo square. On it arrange a portobello mushroom and over it another filo square. Top it with ¼ of the sautéed greens. Continue to layer napoleons in the same way with the remaining ingredients. Warm the assembled napoleons in the preheated 350° oven for 2 minutes.

Pour carrot sauce around each napoleon and top each with a final layer of filo. Garnish with chervil sprigs.

SKATE AND POTATO CAKES WITH TAPENADE

Serves 4

These unusual fish cakes, courtesy of Chef Harding, can be prepared ahead of time and reheated quickly. They are perfect for dinner parties. The *tapenade* and parsley garnish create a leafy crown that emphasizes an indoor garden party flavor.

SKATE CAKES

6 CLOVES GARLIC, UNPEELED

OLIVE OIL

8 OUNCES SKATE FILLET, RAW

2 TABLESPOONS FINELY DICED CARROT

1 TABLESPOON CHOPPED BROAD-LEAF PARSLEY

1 EGG

½ CUP IDAHO GOLD POTATO, STEAMED

2 LARGE BAKING POTATOES

SALT AND FRESHLY GROUND BLACK PEPPER TO TASTE

PARSLEY, TO GARNISH

Preheat oven to 250°. On a sheet of aluminum foil, place garlic and drizzle with olive oil; wrap loosely; bake for 45 minutes; remove; peel and mash. Reserve 1 tablespoon of garlic oil for the skate cakes, discard the rest. Roughly chop the skate and place in a large bowl. Add the carrot, parsley, egg, and Idaho Gold potato, and mix with a fork to break the potato into chunks. Season with salt and pepper.

Peel the baking potatoes and with a *mandoline* cut them into long julienne strips. To make the cakes (four), take 1 ounce of julienned potato and spread like a mat on a plate. Season with salt and pepper. Center 1 ounce (1½ tablespoons) of the skate mixture

on top of the mat of potato strips. Cover with another ounce of the julienned potato. Season. Pat cakes together.

In a sauté pan heat garlic olive oil almost to smoking over high heat. Place skate and potato cake in pan and cook until golden brown, turning with a spatula, about 1½ minutes per side. Remove to paper towels to drain. To warm, place in 350° oven for 3 minutes. Garnish each serving with parsley leaves and *tapenade*.

TAPENADE

1 CUP PITTED BLACK OLIVES, PREFERABLY GREEK

1 TABLESPOON CHOPPED GARLIC

ZEST OF 1 LEMON

2 TABLESPOONS LEMON JUICE

2 TABLESPOONS WATER

4 TABLESPOONS EXTRA-VIRGIN OLIVE OIL

Blend the *tapenade* ingredients in a blender or food processor until smooth.

Humble basketry and food containers used in rural South America, as well as culinary tools, create utilitarian sculpture in a well-stocked kitchen, above.

PASSION FRUIT CUSTARD IN LEMON CUPS

Serves 6

For an elegant dessert, Manna Catering suggests this refreshing and colorful combination, which features a scooped-out lemon as a natural container for passion fruit custard. Its luscious, sweet flavor is set off by tart raspberry sauce. Leaves of mint from your window garden add a finishing touch.

6 LARGE LEMONS

¾ CUP PASSION FRUIT JUICE

6 TABLESPOONS BUTTER

¾ CUP SUGAR

6 EGG YOLKS

1 CUP SLIGHTLY SWEET RASPBERRY PURÉE (RECIPE FOLLOWS)

6 MINT LEAVES FOR GARNISH

Slice the tops off the lemons and carefully scoop out the pulp. Set the shells aside.

In a heavy, 2-quart saucepan combine the passion fruit juice, butter, sugar, and egg yolks. Cook over medium heat, stirring constantly until thickened. Do not let the custard boil. Cool.

Divide the custard among the scooped-out lemon shells and freeze.

Remove from freezer and serve immediately in a pool of the raspberry purée. Garnish with the mint leaves.

FRESH RASPBERRY PUREE

1 PINT FRESH RASP-
BERRIES

2 TABLESPOONS SUGAR
(OR TO TASTE)

In a blender or food processor, puree raspberries, then strain. Add sugar and mix.

Keeping fresh fruits on hand inspires health-minded cooks to concoct tempting dishes, opposite. A wall sculpture of dried botanicals from the herb garden and countryside cheers the kitchen corner.

THE TASTE OF THE OUTDOORS

AUTUMN APPLE CRISP

~~~~~

Serves 6

Soft warm apple slices are hidden under a crumbly topping in this down-to-earth dessert, best enjoyed during apple-picking season. Serve plain or with fresh cream.

5 LARGE COOKING APPLES, PREFERABLY IDA REDS OR GOLDEN DELICIOUS

1 CUP WHOLE WHEAT FLOUR

¾ CUP DARK BROWN SUGAR

¼ CUP TOASTED WHEAT GERM

PINCH OF SALT

½ CUP BUTTER OR MARGARINE AT ROOM TEMPERATURE

CINNAMON

Preheat oven to 375°.

Peel, core, and thickly slice the apples. Put them in a saucepan with ¼ cup water. Cover, and simmer gently for 10 minutes, or until the slices are softened slightly.

Meanwhile, combine the flour, sugar, wheat germ, and salt in a large bowl. Mix together. Add the butter or margarine in chunks. With your fingertips, lightly work the butter into the flour and sugar mixture until you have pea-sized lumps.

Pour the softened apple slices and their juices into a 2-quart baking dish. Sprinkle with cinnamon. Arrange the crumble mixture over apples.

Bake for 35 to 45 minutes, until apple juices begin to bubble over crumble topping. Serve warm or at room temperature.

Potted herbs, a tiered pedestal, and a grain chute recycled as a fruit container make an appealing tableau on a kitchen counter, above.

TROPICAL FRUIT AND SAGE COOLER

Serves 2

A refreshing, sweet-tart beverage with a hint of sage— "sage the saviour," as it was once called, for its medicinal qualities. Although sage is traditionally used to add flavor and aroma to savory dishes, it is actually a member of the mint family and lends itself equally well to fruit dishes and drinks.

2 BANANAS

1 PEAR

6 PINEAPPLE SLICES

¼ LIME

2 TABLESPOONS TOASTED WHEAT GERM

2 CUPS ORANGE JUICE

1 SMALL BUNCH OF SAGE LEAVES (TINY-LEAFED, VARIEGATED SAGE IS USED HERE)

HERB FLOWER ICE CUBES (PROCEDURE FOLLOWS)

Peel and core all the fruit, except the lime, and cut it into chunks. Place in a blender container. Squeeze in the juice of the lime and add the wheat germ, orange juice, and a few sage leaves (about 4 large leaves, or more if they are small), reserving a few leaves for garnish. Blend on high speed until smooth, although tiny pieces of sage leaf may remain. Chill.

Pour into glasses and garnish each glass with a few sage leaves and an herb flower ice cube.

HERB FLOWER ICE CUBES

Pick single flowers of any herb—rosemary, sage, mint, lavender, or thyme—and place one in each compartment of an ice-cube tray. Fill with water and freeze.

Displayed in a spare environment, an edible still-life is particularly striking, right.

SOURCES

UNITED STATES

DESIGNERS AND ARCHITECTS

BENINCASA & McGOWAN DESIGNS
34 Grand Place
East Northport, NY 11731
(516) 368–5117
Interior design and decoration

CENTERBROOK
Box 955
Essex, CT 06426
(203) 767–0175
Architecture

CLODAGH DESIGN
365 First Avenue
New York, NY 10010
(212) 673–9209
Interior design, incorporating
Feng Shui principles

SURA KAYLA
484 Broome Street
New York, NY 10013
(212) 941–8757
Design with living and dried
materials

BOB PATINO
400 East 52 Street
New York, NY 10022
(212) 355–6581
Interior design

VSF
204 West 10 Street
New York, NY 10014
(212) 206–7236
Innovative floral design

MANUFACTURERS/ HANDCRAFTERS

**AURO ORGANIC PAINTS,
SINAN CO. NATURAL
BUILDING MATERIALS**
P.O. Box 857
Davis, CA 95617
(916) 753–3104
Paints and finishes from plant
substances

DECORATOR'S WALK
979 Third Avenue
New York, NY 10022
(212) 355–5300
Natural fiber wallpapers

DONGHIA TEXTILES
979 Third Avenue
New York, NY 10022
(212) 935–3713
Natural fiber wallpapers

JERRY FARRELL
P.O. Box 255
Sidney Center, NY 13839
(607) 369–4916
Contemporary rustic furnishings
made from roots, trunks, and
branches

IRVING & JONES
Village Center
Colebrook, CT 06021
(203) 379–9219
Classic iron garden furnishings

KINGSLEY-BATE
P.O. Box 6797
Arlington, VA 22206
(703) 931–6124
Hand-carved teak garden furniture,
Rainforest Alliance approved

LILYPONS WATER GARDENS
P.O. Box 10
Buckeystown, MD 21717
Recirculating water fountains for
outdoor or indoor use

DANIEL MACK RUSTIC FURNISHINGS
3280 Broadway
New York, NY 10027
(212) 926–3880
Eccentric, contemporary rustic,
peeled or bark-covered items

MASTERWORKS
P.O. Box M, Dept. CD
Marietta, GA 30016
(404) 423–9000
Traditional bent willow furniture

**MOUNT PLEASANT SWEETGRASS
BASKETMAKERS' ASSOCIATION**
P.O. Box 761
Mount Pleasant, SC 29464
Write for purchasing information

THE NATURE OF THINGS
Route 1 Box 157 B3
Viola, WI 54664
Custom-crafted furnishings finished
with barks, shoots, vines, etc.

SMITHSONIAN INSTITUTE COLLECTION
Garden Source Furnishings Inc.
Dept TH
45 Bennett St
Atlanta, GA 30309
Garden furniture reproduced from
originals in the Smithsonian
Institute

TIGER MOUNTAIN WOODWORKS
P.O. Box 249
Scaly Mountain, NC 28775
(704) 526–5577
Twig furniture

VIETRI
(800) 277–5933 for store listings
Hand-thrown terra cotta planters
imported from southern Italy

RETAIL OUTLETS

**CHERCHEZ ANTIQUES &
POTPOURRI LTD.**
862 Lexington Avenue
New York, NY 10021
(212) 737–8215
Scented flower room arrangements

THE COMPLEAT GARDNER
5405 Broadway
San Antonio, TX 78209
(512) 822–0444
Pottery, herbs, perennials, garden
shrubbery, native plants, European
tools, birdhouses and feeders, and
topiary

COUNTRY FLOORS
15 East 16 Street
New York, NY 10003
(212) 627–8300
Stone and terra cotta tiles

**DEVONSHIRE: THE ENGLISH
GARDEN SHOP**
6 N. Madison Street
Middleburg, VA 22117
(703) 687–5990
Fine appointments for the home and
garden bird baths, birdhouses,
animal figures, design books, photo
frames, cachepots, and planters

THE ELEGANT EARTH
1907 Cahaba Road
Birmingham, AL 35223
(205) 870–3264
Unique collection of garden tools,
accessories, and ornaments

FAIRCLOTH & CROKER
P.O. Box 265
Highway 11
South Rising Fawn, GA 30738
(404) 398–2756
American rustic furniture and
birdhouses

THE GARDEN ROOM
8123 Germantown Avenue
Philadelphia, PA 19118
(215) 242–6130
Stone, iron, and terra cotta items
"for the garden and conservatory
of elegance"

THE GARDENER
1836 Fourth Street
Berkeley, CA
(415) 548–4545
Selection of garden tools,
accessories, and furnishings for
indoor or outdoor use

RICHARD KAZARIAN ANTIQUES
70 Charles Street
Boston, MA 02114
(617) 720–2758
Weathered garden antiques

LEXINGTON GARDENS
1008 Lexington Avenue
New York, NY 10021
(212) 861–4390
Garden furnishings and accessories,
many imported

WILLIAM LIPTON/ROBERT HUMA
27 East 61 Street
New York, NY 10021
(212) 593–4341
Decorative barnacles, fungi, etc.

MADDERLAKE
478 Broadway
New York, NY 10013
(212) 941–7770
One-of-a-kind items for garden
or home

MAXILLA & MANDIBLE LTD.
451 Columbus Ave.
New York, NY 10025
(212) 724–6173
Decorative coral, sponges, etc.

LORI PONDER
5221 Wisconsin Avenue, NW
Washington, DC 20015
(202) 537–1010
Garden accessories, books, antiques,
small furniture, original watercolors,
urns and pots, wall hangings, rustic
hutches, birdhouses, furniture, and
perspective trellises

PORTICO
379 West Broadway
New York, NY 10012
(212) 941–7800
Natural furnishings and accessories
from around the world

THE SANTA BARBARA GARDEN
1110 State Street
Santa Barbara, CA 93101
(805) 568–1192
Exterior feeling of interior design:
topiary, statuary, and angels

TERRA VERDE TRADING CO.
72 Spring Street
New York, NY 10012
(212) 925–4533
"Ecological department store" for
the natural home

TURNER MARTIN
540 Emerson Street
Palo Alto, CA
(415) 324–8700
"Living" accessories (moss
sculptures, vegetable topiaries) and
rustic furnishings

VENICE GARDEN FURNITURE
717 California Avenue
Venice, CA 90291
Reproductions of antique garden
furniture, old planters and urns, old
California tile tables, and hand-
wrought furniture

VEEN & POL
399 Bleeker Street
New York, NY 10014
(212) 727–3988
Imported pots and planters, shells,
and baskets

ZONA
97 Greene Street
New York, NY 10012
(212) 925–6750
Natural furnishings and accessories
from around the world

MAIL ORDER

CRATE & BARREL
P.O. Box 3057
Northbrook, IL 60065-3057
Indoor-outdoor furniture, planters,
tableware, etc.

DAVID KAY
1 Jenni Lane
Peoria, IL 61614-3198
(800) 535–9917
Home and garden catalogue

GARDENER'S EDEN
P.O. Box 7307
San Francisco, CA 94120
(415) 421–4242
Garden tools, furniture, and
accessories

THE HERB & SPICE COLLECTION
P.O. Box 118
Norway, IA 52318
(800) 365–4372
Culinary herbs and spices as well as
herbal teas and oils, potpourris,
body-care products, herbal extracts,
and tinctures

THE NATURAL CHOICE
1365 Rufina Circle
Santa Fe, NM 87501
(800) 621–2591
Catalogue includes organic paints,
stains, finishes, and floor treatments

PURE & SIMPLE
124 South Main Street
Box 535
Nashville, AK 71852
(800) 222–5207
Handcrafted indoor-outdoor
furniture in the Southern tradition

SAN FRANCISCO HERB COMPANY
250 14th Street
San Francisco, CA 94103
(800) 227–4530
Full line of spices and potpourri
ingredients; free catalogue

SEVENTH GENERATION
49 Hercules Drive
Colchester, VT 05446
(802) 655–3166
"Green" products for home and
garden

SMITH & HAWKEN
25 Corte Madera
Mill Valley, CA 94941
(415) 383–2000
Garden furnishings and accessories
from plantation and recycled
hardwoods

CULINARY

(Section includes mail-order and retail sources; retail sources are noted.)

ANGELICA HERB & SPICE
147 First Avenue
New York, NY 10009
(212) 677–1549
Dried, edible flowers and herbs

AUX DELICES DES BOIS & FINES HERBES
4 Leonard Street
New York, NY 10014
(212) 334–1230
Fresh herbs, salad greens, and edible flowers

CAMELOT NORTH
2151 Country Road 29
Nisswa, MN 56468
(218) 568–8922
Selection of culinary herb plants, including peppermint, lemon balm, basil and sage; retail only

CATNIP ACRES FARM
67 Christian Street
Oxford, CT 06483-1224
(203) 888–5649
Wide selection of herb plants, including angelica, borage, lemon balm, hyssop, foxglove, and yarrow

THE COOK'S GARDEN
P.O. Box 65
Londonderry, VT 05148-0535
(802) 824–3400
Culinary herb seeds with acclaimed varieties of oregano and basil, including a large-leaved "mammoth" basil that can be used for stuffing poultry and wrapping foods, other herbs, special salad greens, cut flowers, and heirloom and exotic vegetables

CRICKET HILL HERB FARM LTD.
Glen Street
Rowley, MA 01969
(508) 948–2818
Culinary herb blends and potpourri ingredients; catalogue available

THE HERBFARM
32804 Issaquah-Fall City Road
Fall City, WA 98024
(206) 784–2222
Numerous herbal goods, including vinegars, teas, and wreaths

LE JARDIN DU GOURMET
P.O. Box 75
St. Johnsbury Center, VT 05863
(802) 748–1446
Bouquet garni and herb vinegars

PAULA'S CALIFORNIA HERB VINEGARS AND PREMIUM OILS
SWEET ADELAIDE ENTERPRISES, INC.
12918 Cerise Ave.
Hawthorne, CA 90250
(310) 970–7840
Herb vinegars; no-oil salad dressings include basil and orange, lemon and dill, and lime and cilantro; low-sodium herb seasonings

WILLIAMS SONOMA INC.
20 East 60 Street
New York, NY 10022
(212) 980–5155 (retail store)
(800) 541–2233 (mail order)
Items for indoor-outdoor dining, including indoor barbeque grill

UNITED KINGDOM

DESIGNERS AND ARCHITECTS

ATELIER DAMIEN DEWING
Glenholm
George Street
Nailsworth GL6 0AG
0453 834100
Natural furniture and vernacular structures from recycled woods

RODERICK JAMES & CO.
Seagull House
Dittisham Mill Creek
Dartmouth, Devon TQ6 0HZ
Design and construction of oak frame barnhouses

SIMON LYCETT
223 Clapham Road flat 7
London SW9 9BE
071–738–6552
Floral stylist and decorator

NESSA O'NEIL
THE INDOOR GARDEN ROOM
Stratton Audley Hall
Stratton Audley
Oxfordshire OX6 9BT
0869 278256
Interior design, decoration, and planting of indoor garden rooms

MARTIN ROBINSON FLOWERS
637 Fulham Road
London SW6
071–731–3595
Floral and interior design

MANUFACTURERS/ HANDCRAFTERS

ANDREW CRACE DESIGNS
Bourne Lane, Much Hadham
Herts SG10 6ER
027984 2685
Hand-made garden furniture

ANTONIA SPOWERS
Unit 3, Ransome's Dock
35-37 Parkgate Road
London SW11
071–622–3630
Recirculating water fountains

THE ENGLISH BASKET CENTER
The Willows, Curload,
Stoke St. Gregory, Nr. Taunton
Somerset TA3 6JD
0823 69418
Willow basketware and chairs made from own saplings

FIRED EARTH
Middle Aston
Oxfordshire OX5 3PX
0869–40724
Handmade terra cotta tiles

MIKE SMITH
CIRENCESTER WORKSHOPS
Brewery Court
Cirencester Glos GL7 1JH
085–540356
Willow baskets and furnishings from own saplings

RETAIL OUTLETS

ARMSCOTE MANOR DRIED FLOWERS
Armscote, Nr. Stratford on Avon
Warwickshire, CV37 8DA
06–088–2681
Arrangements, topiaries, and potpourris

THE CHAIR COMPANY
180 Wandsworth Bridge Road
London SW6 2VF
071–736–3112
Antique cane and rush

CHELSEA GARDENER
125 Sydney Street
London SW3 6NR
071–352–5656
Garden supplies, including furnishings and water fountains

GREGORY, BOTTLEY & LLOYD
8-12 Rickett Street
London SW6
071–381–5522
Mineralogy and petrology

PATIO LTD.
155 Battersea Park Road
London SW8 4BU
01–622–8262
Huge selection of handmade terra
cotta; global collection of dried
grasses, flowers, seedheads,
potpourris; arrangements also
designed to order

SELSLEA HERB & GOAT FARM
Water Lane
Selslea, Nr. Stroud
Gloucester
0453–766–682
Fresh and dried herbs and aromatic
plants, terracotta planters, dried
herb and flower arrangements,
pomanders and room scenters, and
herbal pillows

MAIL ORDER

**THE FORESTRY COMMISSION
RESEARCH STATION**
Alice Holt Lodge
Wrecclesham, Farnham
Surrey
0420 22255
Pinecones by the sack
(approximately 1,664 cones
per sack).

CULINARY

CARLUCCIO'S
28a Neal Street
London WC2 9PS
071–240–1487
Wide selection of wild mushrooms
and Italian foods.

138

BIBLIOGRAPHY

Colborn, Nigel. *The Container Garden*, Boston: Little Brown, 1990.

Carluccio, Antonio. *A Passion for Mushrooms*. London: Pavilion, 1991.

Docker, Amanda. *An English Country Lady's Book of Dried Flowers*. New York: Doubleday, 1990.

Freeman, Margaret. *Herbs for the Medieval Household*. New York: Metropolitan Museum of Art, 1979.

Mack, Daniel. *Making Rustic Furniture*. New York: Sterling/Lark, 1992.

McHarg, Ian. *Design with Nature*. Garden City: Natural History Press, 1969.

Moore, Charles Willard et al. *The Poetics of Gardens*. Cambridge: Harvard University Press, 1988.

Oliver, Paul. *Dwellings—The House across the World*. Oxford: Phaidon, 1987.

Orbach, Barbara Milo. *The Scented Room: Cherchez's Book of Dried Flowers, Fragrance and Potpourri*. New York: Clarkson Potter, 1986.

Pearson, David. *The Natural House Book: Creating a healthy, harmonious, and ecologically-sound home environment*. New York: Fireside; London: Octopus, 1989.

Rossbach, Sarah. *Interior Design with Feng Shui*. New York: Dutton, 1983.

Progressive Architecture magazine, March '91. Special issue on environmentally conscious architecture and design.

Design Spirit magazine. Alternative design methodology for environmental preservation.

INDEX